Steel as the Answer?

STEEL AS THE ANSWER?

Viking Bodies, Power, and Masculinity in Anglophone Fantasy Literature 2006–2016

Anna Bark Persson

Södertörns högskola

Subject: Gender Studies
Research Area: Critical and Cultural Theory
School of Culture and Education

Södertörns högskola
(Södertörn University)
The Library
SE-141 89 Huddinge

www.sh.se/publications

Cover: Jonathan Robson
Graphic form: Per Lindblom & Jonathan Robson

Stockholm 2023

Södertörn Doctoral Dissertations 216
ISSN 1652–7399
ISBN 978-91-89504-32-5 (print)
ISBN 978-91-89504-33-2 (digital)

Abstract

This dissertation examines the motif of the popular Viking in contemporary Anglophone fantasy literature, with a focus on masculinity, power, embodiment, and sexuality. The study draws on queer-theoretical perspectives on masculinity and the method of queer reading, and approaches the Viking as at once bound up with the legitimization of normative and hegemonic forms of masculinity and open to (queer) negotiations and possibilities beyond normative male masculinities.

The material consists of contemporary gritty fantasy, a recent subgenre deeply invested in contemporary concerns regarding masculinity, masculine failure, and masculinity crisis narratives, where the Viking motif plays a major role. The texts under consideration are Joe Abercrombie's *The First Law* (2006–2012) and *The Shattered Sea* (2014–2015), Richard K. Morgan's *A Land Fit for Heroes* (2008–2016), Mark Lawrence's *The Red Queen's War* (2014–2016), and Elizabeth Bear and Sarah Monette's *The Iskryne Saga* (2007–2015).

Understanding the Viking as a motif that is intractably bound up with ideas of the past and the historical period of the Viking Age but not reducible to it, the thesis considers the fantasy Viking as a medial representation of spectacular hardbody action masculinity and puts it in relation to the fantasy text and fantasy worldbuilding as well as more generalized cultural ideas of the North and the Nordics. Furthermore, it asks how we can understand the masculinity of the Viking – long made symbolic of or associated with white supremacy, misogyny, homophobia, and reactionary gender roles – beyond an assumed direct relation to men or men's concerns.

Analytically, the thesis considers the Viking in relation to spatiality, temporality, and embodiment, finding that in the fantasy text, the Viking emerges with a strong focus on a mighty, muscular body and as a barbarian Other connected to the past and in direct opposition to civilization and futurity, making it an escapist possibility outside the disciplining power of neoliberal late-stage capitalism. Furthermore, connecting to postfeminist perspectives on masculinity in media, the thesis finds that the fantasy Viking has developed in ways that seemingly take into account feminist and queer critique of traditional, homophobic forms of masculinity, transforming the Viking and offering it up for (queer) objectification. At the same time, the Viking also becomes a safe site of traditional masculinity, where anxieties and concerns regarding a supposed loss of male power in modernity can be projected and ultimately resolved.

Keywords: Vikings, the North, the Nordics, masculinity, fantasy literature, queer reading, temporality, postfeminism, embodiment.

Acknowledgements

Completing a PhD degree in Gender Studies has been one of the greatest privileges of my life. That is not to say that it's always been fun or easy, but it has definitely been worthwhile. Strangely, the work of writing a dissertation is on one hand a rather lonely endeavor and on the other utterly dependent upon a large support group of people without whom it would not be possible. As such, the completion of this dissertation owes a number of thanks.

Firstly, to my supervisors Ulla Manns and Ann-Sofie Lönngren, who have guided me through this long and sometimes arduous process with a steady hand. You have both shared your experience, knowledge, skill, time, and patience with me and with this project, and for that I am forever grateful.

Another immense thank you goes to the gender studies collegium at Södertörn University. Being part of this research environment for these past five years has been both fun and enormously rewarding, and I have learned so much from all of you. Thank you to Linn Sandberg, Jenny Sundén, Sam Holmqvist, Ann Werner, Katarina Mattson, Soheyla Yazdanpanah, Helena Hill, Teresa Kulawik, Anna Adeniji, Veronika Muchitsch, Anna Siverskog, Maria Lönn, and Yulia Gradskova. A special thank you goes to my fellow PhD candidates (former and current) for being in this with me: Raili Uibo, Kirill Polkov, Nadia Feshari, Dannie Milwe, Laura Lapinske, and Iwo Nord. Thank you also to my wider network of PhD colleagues: Martin Johansson, Oscar von Seth, Maria Mårsell, Pella Myrstener, and the entire research school of Critical and Cultural Theory. A big thanks also to Jenny Karlsson, Ewa Rogström, and Elina Nylander for your assistance in making all the administrative parts of being a PhD run smoothly.

My PhD position was funded by Nordforsk through the research hub *Reimagining Norden in an Evolving World* (ReNEW). Thank you for finding my project intriguing, and for providing the support and infrastructure I needed to step into the field of studies on the Nordics, which was completely new to me. A special thank you goes to Norbert Götz, Peter Stadius, Tuire Liimatainen, Nina Carlsson, Frederik Forrai Ørskov, and Steffan Werther.

This project is also greatly indebted to Jenny Björklund. Mostly because she was my 90% opponent and gave me valuable feedback at a critical phase of the project. Additionally, Jenny has been my teacher since my very first steps into the field of gender studies in Uppsala 2013, supervised my master thesis, and was a big supporter when I applied for PhD positions. A big thank you for your continued support and encouragement!

Another thank you goes to my two commentators on the 90% text, Christopher Collstedt and Ann Werner. Thank you, Kalle Berggren, my 60% opponent, who provided a very helpful reading at an earlier stage, helping my refine and rework the project at a crucial moment. I also want to extend an extra thanks to Jenny Sundén, my third reader, for helping me with the very final part of the writing stage.

Thanks are also required to the Fantasy Online Research Seminar (FORS) and to Stefan Ekman for organizing it, providing a constructive space to discuss fantasy criticism and theory. I'm grateful also to the Higher Seminar in Literature at Södertörn University for inviting me to both present and partake. Alongside the PhD studies, I also worked as editorial assistant for *Tidskrift för genusvetenskap* at Uppsala University. Thank you, editors Karin S. Lindelöf and Camilla Flodin for all you've taught me about publishing and academia.

Outside the professional sphere, my friends and close ones also have provided unending support during this process. Thank you Hanna Olofsdotter for always being there. Thank you Johan Jönsson, for encouraging me to write, and for all your letters – enjoy that archive of doctoral anxiety in return! Thank you also for reading an early draft of the dissertation and providing helpful comments on all the fantasy stuff.

Thank you to Veronica Green for writing support, dinner company, and for always keeping me appraised about what Jordan B Peterson is up to. Thank you Nahal Ghanbari for all the tea, the late-night talks, and for always telling me how much you look forward to a friend completing a dissertation in a subject that is not incomprehensible.

Thank you to David Ling and Katja Byström for all your support and advice – and a special thanks to David to agreeing to work out with me in the mornings, even though you hated it. Thank you Sara Westerdahl for all the dinners. Thank you Maria Nygård for being an excellent librarian and giving me really good recommendations for Nordic and Viking fantasy. Thank you Daniel Albertsson for offloading a bunch of fantasy theory on me.

A big thank you goes also to Anna Davour, Amelie Rahbek, Madeleine Eriksson, Tobias Holmberg, Alex Lindqvist, Lukas Bengtsson de Veen, Ingrid Holmström, Sivan Måwe, Brith and Birger Holmström, Frida Persson, Gustav Andersson, Mikael Persson and Margareta Bark.

Thank you also to the SFF fandom, for the community and friends I found there, and for being my first guide in literary analysis. Thank you also to the anonymous contributors to the *First Law* and *A Land Fit for Heroes* wikis, allowing me to quickly look up details during writing, as well as the members of the Facebook group Svenska sf- och fantasyfans for always replying to my random questions about Vikings in fantasy and for giving me plenty of reading suggestions.

The final thank you goes, of course, to Karin Holmström, for everything. I love you tera much.

Contents

Chapter 1: Introduction

In the fantasy novel *Red Country*, by British author Joe Abercrombie, a character hires a writer to chronicle his adventurous journeys through the fantasy world. However, the writer, looking "for a tale to stir the blood", seems more intrigued by the ravages of a nearby Viking or Northman, leaving the would-be historic adventurer to bitterly complain: "No doubt I'll end up the villain in the book I commissioned while yonder decapitating madman is celebrated to the rafters!" (Abercrombie 2013, 401) Much like the fickle writer in *Red Country*, this book is concerned with precisely this decapitating madman: the Viking as a blood-stirring, violent warrior figure that seems to command endless fascination and popularity.

What a Viking is, exactly, is a question under constant discussion,[1] with history, archeology, and the popular imagination providing different answers. Particularly in the case of the popular Viking, the answer to what a Viking is seems closely connected to traditional and reactionary discourses on white masculinity. As Katherine J. Lewis puts it: "Popular perceptions of the Vikings have long held them to be the epitome of an unbridled form of hypermasculinity predicated on physical strength, born of impressive musculature, and callous brutality. They rape women and bend lesser men to their will." (Lewis 2019, 5) In this current moment of growing right-wing extremism and fascism, faced with a supposed crisis in masculinity where many white men perceive themselves as losing ground in an increasingly feminized, queer-friendly, and multi-cultural world, the Viking seems a direct recourse to an imaginary past of cultural homogeneity and reassuringly masculine pursuits.

Consider, for example, the 'Viking Guy' from the storming of Capitol Hill in January 2021 in protest against Donald Trump's defeat in the 2020 US election. Decked out in pelts, horns, and with a Thor's hammer and a *valknut*[2] tattooed on his chest, 'Viking Guy' was prominently displayed in the ensuing media footage as he rampaged through the Capitol. Or The Golden One, a Swedish Neo-Nazi YouTuber flexing his 'Viking' physique in front of his

---

[1] Evident already in my hedging between the categories of the 'Viking' and the 'Northman' above, a lack of distinction that will be further discussed below.

[2] An old Norse symbol that is increasingly being used in white supremacist contexts.

many viewers, while encouraging them to train for the coming war to defend Western civilization – and to buy protein powder from his own label, named *Jotunheim*.[3]

A symbol of masculinity, might, and whiteness, the Viking has a long history of association with fascist, racist, and (neo-)Nazi discourse and organizing. At the same time, the Viking is a figure of wide cultural appeal, and the last decade has seen a veritable Viking boom in the media, with History Channel's tv-series *Vikings* (2013–2020) and *Vikings: Valhalla* (2022–), blockbuster action film *The Northman* (2022), and popular video games like *Assassin's Creed: Valhalla* (2020). Here the Viking takes a familiar shape of something warlike, tough, manly, and bloodthirsty, but has also been broadened to make room for other ways of envisioning Viking Age society – taking into account the domestic sphere, women's perspectives and roles, trade, or queer sexualities. With the new discovery regarding the Birka grave Bj 581[4] as well as a long-standing idea of Viking Age society as more gender equal than many other parts of history, the idea of the Viking also includes feminist investments about strong women in history and 'girl power' discourses of female warriors (Williams 2019; Rosenström and Žiačková 2022).

Furthermore, the Viking and its popular uses have been subject to intense critique from feminist as well as other critical perspectives, looking to deconstruct its association with masculinity and war, its ties to masculinist and fascist discourses, as well as the very concept of 'Viking' itself. Within historical and archeological research, the popular Viking generally emerges as a problem to be critiqued and rectified, a misinformed construction of an historical time that never was (see Williams 2016). Archeologists Gudrun Whitehead and Barbora Žiačková have both considered the popular reception of Viking Age history and the idea of the Viking, and argue that increasingly, the Viking is losing its specificity, being severed from its Norse-Germanic origins, and emerging instead as a more general image of strength, masculinity, and whiteness (Whitehead 2014, 49–50; Žiačková 2019, 1). The Viking is a phantasmagoric figure, its popular instantiation deriving as much – if not more – from mythology, fiction, and fantasy, as historical fact (Cederlund 2011).

---

[3] The realm of the giants in Norse mythology.

[4] A grave first excavated in the 19th century believed to be of a male warrior, was in 2017 through a genomic analysis confirmed to hold biologically female bones (Hedenstierna-Jonson et al. 2017), which prompted a flurry of news stories about 'Viking women warriors' (see for example: Glover 2017; O'Neill 2017; Vagianos 2017).

The Golden One records many of his videos sitting in front of a well-stocked bookcase, with Tolkien's *Lord of the Rings* as well as more recent fantasy titles like Abercrombie's books prominently displayed. The storming of Capitol Hill, with the shamanic, fantastic figure of 'Viking Guy' among them, quickly saw a video reply from actor, Republican politician, and bodybuilder Arnold Schwarzenegger. Iconic for his action film roles, Schwarzenegger in the video brandishes Conan's[5] sword, using it as a metaphor for how the US will be rebuilt stronger than ever before once this threat against its democracy is defeated. Viking Age history, the Eddas, Icelandic Sagas, and medieval literature have been important and enduring inspirations for the kind of genre fantasy these images are drawn from, but fundamental to this thesis is that these current uses of the Viking – particularly in relation to narratives of the decline of (white) men – in turn also draw closely on fantasy literature, on both its construction of the Viking, and its narrative logic.

Significantly, fantasy developed as a literary mass-market genre from the popular success of *Lord of the Rings*, written by medievalist J.R.R. Tolkien as an attempt to resurrect the medieval saga for the modern world. As such, fantasy literature lies close to the epic and its characters to the exteriorized heroic than the 'everyday' and present of the contemporary novel.[6] The Viking is similarly an epic figure, in every sense of the word. As much as a particular historical time and place, the Viking is associated with a narrative of struggle, battle, might, and war. The popular Viking represents or imagines a masculine power forged in the berserker rage of the battlefield, the crush of the shield wall, the co-mingling of jubilation and dread in the face of a Ragnarök;[7] it is not an image of the everyday, but of the epic, historic, *storied*. In short, a power fantasy – with emphasis on the fantasy.

---

[5] Conan the Barbarian was a fantasy hero created by Robert Howard in 1932 and originated in sword and sorcery pulp magazines. The stories have been adapted many times, most notably in the 1982 movie starring Schwarzenegger in the titular role. Conan is not a Viking figure but draws on similar constructions of the savage Northman (see Young 2016, 26), a figure I will discuss further below.

[6] This distinction I derive from Mikhail Bakhtin's "Epic and Novel: Towards a Methodology for the Study of the Novel" (1941). In the essay, Bakhtin outlines and contrasts the properties of the novel with that of the epic. The novel is not poetic, its hero is not heroic and is not static but develops during the course of the text, and the novel is concerned with the present and the everyday. This is very different from the epic, which is separated from its present by an epic distance, concerned with a legendary and idealized past and the supposedly eternal. The same goes for its hero, who is externalized and complete in the text. The popular fantasy text draws heavily on the epic, but it is also shaped by the novel and "combines the mimetic and fantastic modes", according to Brian Attebery (1992, 72).

[7] An eschatological event of Norse mythology, Ragnarök is the time when the gods die and the world is submerged into water, eventually to rise again.

While important, the close focus on critique and deconstruction of what is viewed as highly problematic masculine imagery, the supposed normativity and heterosexuality of the Viking and the Viking body, has been left intact. It has also left the wider complexities of the pleasurable appeal of this popular image of muscular male power largely unexamined. Via contemporary fantasy literature dealing closely with various crises of masculinity and the breakdown of masculine power, autonomy, and the male body itself through the use of the Viking motif, I approach the Viking through a queer reading, focusing foremost on how the Viking body relates to power and sexuality. Approaching the Viking from a queer perspective means not only excavating its queer potentialities, but also examining why and how it emerges as such a prevailing phantasmic figure of male power.

Aim and Research Questions

The aim of this study is to, through a reading of contemporary fantasy literature, examine the popular Viking in relation to sexuality, masculinity, and power. More specifically, I am interested in the Viking as a shorthand for masculinity and (male) power, and how the Viking relates to contemporary concerns regarding masculinity and power. Both in the case of the Viking as a site in need of feminist and anti-racist critique and its usage as a solid touchstone of reassuringly manly masculinity, of a properly masculine past in contrast to the supposedly emasculating present, the Viking comes to embody and represent extreme forms of traditional masculinity. Here sexuality and heteronormativity become a way of approaching the Viking and the Viking body to understand how the Viking relates to masculinity and power in a wider sense, beyond simply a retrenched retreat to traditional or conservative forms of manhood.

Emerging from an understanding of masculinity as at once closely related to normativity, legitimacy, and empowerment, and also a possible site of queerness open to appropriation and transformation, I ask foremost not how the popular Viking reproduces misogynistic and racist notions, but rather what this very particular form of heterosexual hardbody masculinity does and what possibilities it engenders. Turning to contemporary fantasy literature as both a place where these Viking images proliferate (and, in turn, inspire mainstream understandings of the Viking), and a speculative literary space where it might be more open to flux and change, I seek to answer the following questions:

- What can a queer-theoretical reading of the popular Viking, focused on sexuality and embodiment, offer for understanding masculinity?
- What is the function of the Viking in the fantasy text?
- What ideas of masculinity, sexuality, power, and embodiment does the popular Viking mobilize?

Vikings, Northmen, and Northern Barbarians

As a popular motif, the Viking is at once an immediately recognizable figure and in a state of constant mutability and flux. Andrew Wawn argues that it is because of the Viking's "capacity to undergo cultural translation and modernization" that it has become such a cultural mainstay (Wawn 2000, 371). In *The Viking and the Victorians: Inventing the Old North in 19th Century Britain* (2000), Wawn traces how scholarly and cultural fascination with ideas of the 'Old North' in Victorian Britain invented and popularized the term *Viking*. Furthermore, while this fascination initially derived from historical sources and medieval literature, it soon developed in what Wawn calls "an instance of the kind of spray-on old northern atmospherics still favored today by Scandinavian lottery operators, Icelandic saga publishers, French manufacturers of baby clothes, American vodka distillers, film producers and golf course designers" (Wawn 2000, 5). Wawn here points to two important things. Firstly, the slippery space between the idea of the Viking, the (Old) North, and a more general Northman motif. Secondly, the immense commercial and popular attraction of the Viking, whose 'exotic' Nordic appeal can be made to sell almost anything (see also Andersen et al. 2019; Dale 2020). Carl Olof Cederlund, too, points to this general applicability of the term Viking. While it appears a rather specific term, ostensibly referring to the people who lived in Scandinavia in 793–1066 AD, it has also long been used in reference to "ancient Nordic times in general" (Cederlund 2011, 21). The idea of the Viking is directly connected both to ideas of the North and the Nordics more generally, and to the closely related motifs of the Northman and the Northern barbarian.

The idea of the Northman or the Northern barbarian is an historical construct going back to Antiquity, when the territories and people north of the Roman Empire were interpreted as wild and barbaric in relation to Roman civilization. This figure of the Northman or the Germanic barbarian was thus initially created by a superior imperial power who portrayed them as at once noble savages and ultimately inferior (Lönnroth 2017, 13–14). Lill Eilertsen sums up this figure as "an old European mythological construct of 'the independent and freedom loving character of Northmen'. This construct is rooted in classical literature [...] as well as a tenacious belief in the interdependency of elements, climate and human temperament, in accordance with proto-psychological theories of humorism [...]" (Eilertsen 2012, 189). Throughout history, the motif of the Northman or Northern barbarian has gone through many changes, shaped, as Lars Lönnroth writes, "by Roman and Christian poetics, chivalric literature, Goethean nationalism and romanticism, Wagnerian opera, Nazi ideology, and, last but not least, mass-produced fantasy" (Lönnroth 2017, 173 [my translation]).

The connection between the idea of the Viking and "mass-produced fantasy" regularly shows up in research on the popular Viking. Examining Viking motifs in historical fiction, Lisa Bennett and Kim Wilkins sum up and dismiss fantasy as fiction that "continues to gain pleasure from the monstrous northern Other (who is mapped onto wastelands and jagged mountain peaks inside front covers)" – in contrast to contemporary historical fiction that instead attempts to develop and humanize this figure in various ways (Bennett and Wilkins 2019, 3). Björn Sundmark, giving an historical overview of Vikings in children's literature, makes a brief foray into fantasy literature. Citing J.R.R. Tolkien's *Lord of the Rings* (1954) and Poul Anderson's *The Broken Sword* (1954), he writes that they "pay more oblique homage to Viking legends and saga traditions [...] Tolkien's and Anderson's Nordic-inspired fantasies are original and innovative. These are works that exploit and expand the narrative potential of Nordic culture and religion" (Sundmark 2014, 206–207). However, he does not explore this any further.

While the influences of the Old North and Nordic medieval literature on the formation of fantasy as a literary genre is well-established (see for example Shippey 1982; Arvidsson 2007), the fantasy Viking itself has not attracted much scholarly attention. Turning to fantasy literature to read the popular Viking means rectifying this, but, more importantly, I am interested in fantasy literature precisely because of the obliqueness Sundmark mentions. Žiačková writes that currently "the meaning of 'Viking' has shifted and become emblematic of a particular type of hyper-masculinity – the image of a white, bearded warrior – allowing it to extend beyond Scandinavian-Germanic ethnicity [...]" (Žiačková 2019, 1). This conceptual promiscuity of the term 'Viking' – covering both an historical specificity connected to Viking Age Scandinavia, a more general Northman or Nordic barbarian, a general sense of Nordicness, and even simply just an image of straight, white, warrior masculinity – is central to this thesis, but also, I would argue, for fantasy literature. While drawing inspiration from history, fantasy after all is concerned with the unreal and the building of fictious worlds (Ekman and Taylor 2016) and the Vikings found in fantasy literature are drawn from a wide array of influences (as I will show in chapter two). Importantly, this study is concerned with the Viking not foremost as an historical motif, but rather a popular or mass medial image revolving around certain ideas of masculinity, sexuality, power, and embodiment.

Gritty Fantasy and Fantasy as Speculative Fiction

This study turns to popular fantasy for three reasons. One, because fantasy literature is an under-researched form of media where Viking images proliferate. Two, because fantasy literature, as a form of speculative fiction, may help open up novel ways to think about the problematic figure of the Viking. And third, because contemporary popular epic fantasy is intimately invested in the questions of masculinity, sexuality, power, autonomy, and masculinity crises that I am interested in here.

Fantasy is a broad literary genre, which, depending on the definition, may encompass any form of literature that deals with the unreal (Hume 1984, 21). Here I am mainly interested in popular fantasy or genre fantasy,[8] particularly a recent form of it often referred to as *gritty fantasy* (or *grimdark*). Gritty fantasy is a subset or development of epic fantasy,[9] initially developed in the early 2000s, inspired by Glen Cook's *The Black Company* (1984) and George R.R. Martin's *A Song of Ice and Fire* (1998–), as well as roleplaying games, sword and sorcery, video games, and film – particularly action and war films. Helen Young defines gritty fantasy as "marked by low-levels of magic, high-levels of violence, in-depth character development, and medievalist worlds that are 'if not realistic, at least have pretensions to realism' in their depictions

---

[8] Here understood mainly in terms of what Gary K. Wolfe describes as a "functional, largely commonsense approach to genre", that its given readership approach as "something more than a sales category but perhaps less than an art form distinct from the general arts of fiction" (Wolfe 2011, 2). See also Farah Mendlesohn and Edward James' formulation of a "short" history of fantasy (Mendlesohn and James 2009).

[9] Brian Stableford defines epic fantasy as commercialized fantasy following *Lord of the Rings* in the use of a secondary fantasy world and in drawing inspirations from the epics: "the primary model of commodified fantasy retains and exemplifies many of the pretensions as well as the narrative formula of the epic [...] they gradually build up detailed historical and geographical images of secondary worlds, within which elaborate hero myths are constructed" (Stableford 2009, 130–31). Stableford understands the 'epic' of the epic fantasy in two ways: firstly, in terms of scope – these are long-ranging series consisting of many substantial instalments that work to produce a large and detailed secondary fantasy world – and secondly, in terms of the inspiration it borrows from the epic as a literary mode. To apply Wolfe's functional sense of genre (see note 8), it is the kind of fantasy literature most people think of when they hear "fantasy".

of rain, blood, and mud" (Young 2016, 63). Gritty fantasy has generally been understood as a turn away from an earlier form of mass market fantasy often referred to as *post-Tolkienian* – works closely inspired by Tolkien's *Lord of the Rings* and his generally romantic and chivalric view of the medieval. In "Dreaming of the Middle-Ages" (1995), Umberto Eco categorizes Western popular obsession with the medieval into several different forms. Put in his terms, gritty fantasy substitutes the "Middle Ages of *Romanticism*" of earlier fantasy for "The Middle Ages as a *barbaric* age, a land of elementary and outlaw feelings" (Eco 1995, 69 [emphasis in original]).

Gritty fantasy has also been understood as an ironic, metatextual deconstruction of earlier forms of fantasy, particularly when it comes to the fantasy hero, masculinity, and chivalry (Sedlmayr 2014; Polack 2015; Petzold 2017; Carroll 2018). Gerold Sedlmayr reads the incessant violence of gritty fantasy and its continuous breakdown or mutilation of the (male) body as a critique of body politics in late-stage capitalism (Sedlmayr 2014), while Jochen Petzold understands it as a nihilistic deconstruction of heroism, in which heroics is both impossible to achieve and impossible *not* to attempt in a never-ending circle of failure and impotency (Petzold 2017). Shiloh Carroll, writing on George R.R. Martin, reads his work as "show[ing] how poisonous a society that devalues women and glorifies strength of arms can be" by portraying chivalry as "a masquerade behind which 'true' masculinity – violent, aggressive, and misogynist – hides" (Carroll 2018, 56). The breakdown and feebleness of the male body and its continuous failure are also hallmarks of typical masculinity crisis narratives in media and popular culture (see for example Green and Madison 2013; Gill 2014). Instead of understanding gritty fantasy foremost as a response to earlier forms of fantasy, I place it in a wider context of representations of masculinity, particularly in relation to ideas of failed masculinity and narratives of masculinity in crisis.

I also place gritty fantasy into a wider context of speculative fiction. Science fiction has long been recognized as speculative space, ripe with possibilities for feminist reimaginings, particularly in relation to gender, sexuality, technology, and embodiment (Haraway 1991; 1997; Rose 1994; Pearson, Hollinger, and Gordon 2008). Furthermore, science fiction has been understood as a particularly salient literature of the 21st century: science fiction author Kim Stanley Robinson has often referred to SF as the "realism of our times", while Istvan Csicsery-Ronay writes that "sf is ingrained within the quotidian consciousness of people living in the postindustrial world"; it is about "the relationship between imaginary conceptions and historical reality unfolding into the future" (Csicsery-Ronay Jr. 2008, 5, 4; see also Jameson 2005).

Fantasy, on the other hand, has instead tended to be viewed in terms of nostalgia and conservatism, a childish longing for a past that never was and for fairytale comforts divorced from reality (Suvin 1979/2016, 37; Miéville 2002; see also Tolkien 1997). Fantasy literature can certainly be conservative and reactionary, but is, like science fiction, a genre where rumination of temporality and, in particular, modernity and post-modernity are central concerns – albeit from different temporal horizons in-text. Where science fiction extends from the present into the future (Csicsery-Ronay Jr. 2008, 81), fantasy instead generally extends from the present into the past. Kim Gordon understands the fantasy genre's preoccupation with medievalism as a critique of Western late modernity, its creation of an Edenic, escapist medieval realm where "good and evil are clearly delineated" (Gordon 2004, 2) as part of an "'anti-modern' impetus" (ibid., 3). Gritty fantasy, significantly, goes in the opposite direction, extending from the imaginary medieval past into the present.

Central to fantasy, and to speculative fiction generally, is the world. Hanna-Riikka Roine argues that worldbuilding is a fundamental rhetorical practice of speculative fiction, writing that

> [t]he true power of speculative fiction lies not in the invention of a speculative premise or speculative beings, but in the way the abstract premise (or a model of world) is concretised in the framework built for working it through. In this, it is a form of communicating ideas, or bringing new ideas up for discussion. […] I see speculative worldbuilding as a way of turning abstract and general thought experiments (or ideas) into a particular and therefore communicable form. (Roine 2016, 16, 19)

She further writes that "speculative fiction, in particular, relies on literalisation of metaphorical expressions" (Roine 2016, 18).[10] In short, Roine argues that because speculative fiction premieres the literal over the metaphorical, the fictive worlds constructed by speculative fiction become a way to concretely work through ideas.

Medievalism in gritty fantasy has tended to be examined either in terms of a masculinist fantasy of a return to an imaginary time of traditional gender relations and racial homogeneity (Kaufman 2016; Young 2016), or as a

---

[10] Compare to Adam Roberts, who writes: "Instead of abstract, SF texts prefer the concrete, so, rather than meditate upon 'alienness', a SF novel is more likely to present us with an actual concretely realised alien, with blue skin and bug eyes." (Roberts 2000, 14)

popular conceptualization of a specific historic period (Larrington 2015; Carroll 2018). Taking the medievalist world and its temporality as the point from which the gritty fantasy text unfolds, means attending to what the medieval is used to construct or communicate on the level of worldbuilding. Where the traditional post-Tolkienian fantasy is static and unchanging, always returning to a status quo located in a glorious past, the gritty fantasy is instead set in a medieval past clearly moving towards something akin to the present, suspended in a moment where the medieval is slowly and inexorably giving way to modernity.[11]

In works like *Discipline and Punish* (1975) and *The History of Sexuality* (1976), Michel Foucault operationalizes a medieval/modern distinction so as to make comprehensible and demonstrate shifts in the operation of power and knowledge over time. Carolyn Dinshaw writes that for Foucault, the medieval functions at once as "a period that produces our modernity, and as a period quite separate and different from our own" (Dinshaw 1999, 200). She describes Foucault's use of the medieval as "utopian [...] elegiac [...] nostalgic" (Dinshaw 1999, 200), and understands Foucault as "fictioning history" as part of his radical politics (ibid., 205). Following this, I have argued elsewhere (Bark Persson 2022) that the gritty fantasy through its worldbuilding enacts something akin to the Foucauldian medieval/modern divide, making meaningful different formulations of power as they come into contact with each other. Gritty fantasy is, I would argue, intensely preoccupied with operations of power. It places the absolute power of kings next to the supposedly sovereign body of the hero, and, significantly, a budding capitalist system that becomes symbolic of regulatory or disciplinary forms of power as well as economic rationality (see Sedlmayr 2014, 172; cf Eco 1995, 64).

Science fiction, with its future-oriented horizons, has been fruitful in supplying a vernacular for thinking and grappling with technological change, futurity and progress, hybridity, and the breakdown of supposedly stable and given categories like the natural, the body, or the subject (Haraway 1991). Gritty fantasy, on the other hand, extending from the present into the past and back again, offers a very different set of speculative possibilities. Concerned with the medieval/modern divide and focused on the world and

---

[11] I base this shift in fantasy temporality on Farah Mendlesohn's distinction of what she calls *the portal-quest fantasy* and *the immersive fantasy*: "Where the portal-quest fantasies emphasized recognition and healing, the restoration of the grandeur of previous days, the immersive fantasies are overwhelmingly concerned with the entropy of the world." (Mendlesohn 2008, 60–61) See Bark Persson (2022) for further discussion.

the epic before the interpersonal or subjective,[12] gritty fantasy provides certain ways of making governance and power visible and meaningful in particular ways, played out in the tension between medieval power systems, encroaching modernity (here defined in terms of the Foucauldian medieval/modernity dichotomy), and the (supposedly) sovereign hero that is the fantasy character (see Attebery 1992, 73, 86; Petzold 2017, 135; Bark Persson 2022). The Viking, and in particular his strong and muscular body, is, as we shall see in the analysis, closely bound together with these contrasting and contrary formulations of power.

Theoretical Formulations: Masculinity and Power

The guiding theoretical concept underlying my reading of the Viking is *masculinity*, not in order to essentialize what the idea of the Viking is, but because the idea of the Viking is inexplicably bound up with ideas of masculinity. Kalle Berggren, arguing for a sustained incorporation of feminist poststructuralist and phenomenological perspectives in masculinity studies, has suggested understanding masculinity in terms of *stickiness*. Drawing on Sara Ahmed, he points to stickiness as a way "to have it both ways and to avoid the false choice between discourse, norms, and power on one hand, and bodies, emotions and lived experience on the other" (Berggren 2014, 245). He writes:

> Bodies culturally read as 'men' are oriented toward the culturally established signs of 'masculinity,' such as hardness and violence. The repeated sticking together of certain bodies and signs in this way is what creates masculine subjectivity. This is always a contested, variable, and uncertain process, but one in which the repeated enactment of masculinity tends to be sticky and naturalized [...]. (ibid.)

I approach the Viking in a similar manner: as a motif that sticks to masculinity and to which masculinity sticks, predicated upon hardness and violence, as well as certain ideas of the male body.

As previously laid out, the connection between the idea of the Viking and masculinity is firmly established in the popular imagination. It is also consistently challenged, both by historical and archeological research, and

---

[12] Brian Attebery writes: "Fantastic tales are generally seen as naive or artless because they emphasize story over verbal texture and depth of characterization." (Attebery 1992, 54) To this centrality of story, later scholars have also added the importance of world (see Mendlesohn 2008; Ekman 2013; Roine 2016).

critiques against the usage of Viking symbolism for reactionary ends. Understanding the Viking in relation to masculinity as sticky means taking into account this relationship as "contested, variable, and uncertain", rather than automatic or naturalized. Instead of approaching the Viking as some sort of archaic or primeval form of masculinity leading back into a masculine past, I instead see this motif as consistently invested in as masculine figure. In turn, this investment also reproduces very specific established ideas of masculinity, men, and male bodies, centering them around "hardness and violence".

Within the field of masculinity studies, the linkages between men, the male body, masculinity, and power have been interrogated, complicated, and pried apart in various ways. Fundamentally, Raewyn Connell's influential concept of hegemonic masculinity posits patriarchal power as legitimized by certain ways of doing masculinity, and access to hegemonic forms of masculinity and power as predicated upon class, race, and sexuality (Connell 2008). Masculinity research has focused on men's lived experiences, discursive constructions of masculinity, and structural perspectives, understanding masculinity as intersectional and plural, as well as situational (Kimmel, Hearn, and Connell 2005; Gottzén and Jonsson 2012; Gottzén, Mellström, and Shefer 2020).

Queer-theoretical approaches to masculinity, on the other hand, have focused in particular ways on embodiment and power. Specifically, queer approaches to masculinity have revolved around deconstructing and reconfiguring masculine embodiment, as well as severing the presupposition of a direct and naturalized link between masculinity and men. These theoretical contributions include a focus on female and non-male bodied masculinities (Halberstam 1998), as well as the deconstruction of the naturalness of the heterosexual male body. Through centering queer sexual practices and attending to the potential receptiveness of the male body – as opposed to the impenetrability valued and presupposed from the view of hegemonic heterosexual masculinity – queer approaches to men and masculinity attempt to queer and disturb normative understandings of masculinity (Bersani 1987; Waldby 1995; Thomas 2002).

In "Destruction: Boundary Erotics and Refigurations of the Heterosexual Male Body" (1995), Catherine Waldby writes:

> The culture's privileging of masculinity means that the hegemonic bodily imago of masculinity conforms with his status as sovereign ego, the destroyer [...] The male body is understood as phallic and impenetrable, as a war-body

> simultaneously armed and armoured, equipped for victory. The female body is its opposite, permeable and receptive, able to absorb all this violence. (Waldby 1995, 268)

Queer interventions in masculinity seek to deconstruct this idea of the phallic and impenetrable male war-body and this binary, heteronormative construction of gender, which we, with Judith Butler (1990), can refer to as *the heterosexual matrix*. Butler defines the heterosexual matrix as a "discursive/epistemic model of gender intelligibility that assumes that for bodies to cohere and make sense there must be a stable sex expressed through a stable gender [...] that is oppositionally and hierarchically defined through the compulsory practice of heterosexuality" (Butler 1990/2006, 208). Gender is produced through the cultural mandate that a body gendered as female expresses femininity and desires bodies gendered as male that express masculinity and vice versa.

Following the heterosexual matrix, masculinity then is the set of bodily practices, behaviors, and desires that emerge in opposition to, hierarchically superior to, and supposedly complementary to the bodily practices, behaviors, and desires coded feminine; masculinity is the discursive, cultural and subjective identificatory practices that express and gender the body as male, in an oppositional and dialectical relationship to femininity and bodies produced as female in the hegemonic gendering of bodies and identities. However, even as bodies gain comprehensibility and legitimacy through to the supposed stable linkages of body–gender–desire, there is no given or natural affinity between masculinity and the male body or femininity and the female body, according to Butler, but is rather something that needs to be continually performed and reproduced.

In *Female Masculinity* (1998) Jack Halberstam argues that it is precisely through insisting that non-male bodies cannot perform masculinity or do so faultily that male power is naturalized and safe-guarded. Halberstam looks closer at female and FTM[13] masculinities not as imitations of dominant forms of masculinity, but rather as viable alternatives to it, writing:

> Masculinity in this society inevitably conjures up notions of power and legitimacy and privilege; it often symbolically refers to the power of the state and uneven distributions of wealth. Masculinity seems to extend outward into patriarchy and inward into the family; masculinity represents the power of

---

[13] Short for "female to male", used for describing trans men and trans masculine subjects' transitions towards masculinity.

> inheritance, the consequences of the traffic in women, and the promise of
> social privilege. But, obviously, many other lines of identification traverse the
> terrain of masculinity, dividing its power into complicated differentials of
> class, race, sexuality, and gender. (Halberstam 1998, 2)

Halberstam separates female masculinities from male masculinities, especially its most privileged forms, and argues for a complex understanding of the
relationship between masculinity and power. Furthermore, Halberstam
understands masculinity as a symbolic referent for all forms of (patriarchal)
power, at the same time as the connection between masculinity and power is
complicated by intersectional categories such as class, sexuality, race, and
gender.

In *Masculinity Without Men? Female Masculinity in Twentieth-Century
Fictions* (2004), Jean Bobby Noble criticizes what they consider to be
Halberstam's too quick severance of masculinity and power. They write:

> each subject of female masculinity I theorize is bound by the materialization
> of manhood as it appears in and is, as it were, spoken through different classes,
> races, sexualities, and bodies [...] [and] interested in taking up power
> precisely in and as masculine power. Each of my subjects finds power not by
> feigning indifference but, rather, by cultivating proximity, identification, and
> similarity with other subjects of masculinity [...] Masculinity, regardless of
> what type of body it is articulated through, by definition marks a space of
> proximity with men [...]. (Noble 2004, xl, xlii)

In queer theoretical understandings of masculinity, masculinity is at once
pluralistic and intersectional, always possibly queer, and existing beyond the
sole confine of the male, heterosexual body. Even so, these forms of alternate
or subordinate masculinities are put in relation to the cultural construction
and, above all, the cultural privileging of heterosexual, white, middle-class
masculinity and forms of embodiment associated with it. Here, masculinity
is symbolically and culturally closely connoted with power and legitimacy,
even as access to that power and legitimacy is conditioned upon being male,
white, affluent, and straight – which, according to Noble, can never be completely divorced from a certain form of "materialization of manhood".

This I read not as an essentializing claim that only 'real' men, whatever
that may mean, can truly have access to masculinity, but rather that con-
ceptualizing, relating to, or performing masculinity in some sense always
proceeds from normative understandings or imaginaries of the male body –
as well as the ideas of power bound up with masculinity and male embodi-

ment in Western culture more generally. Put differently, masculinity and male bodies, to return to Berggren, stick together. Noble, then, understands masculinity not as an inherent quality of male bodies, but, importantly, as an identity, lived experience, and set of practices and codes that are culturally and symbolically entwined with men and accessed through proximity with men and ideas about heteronormative manhood – much like the Viking.

Following Halberstam and Noble's consideration of non-male masculinities, I understand masculinity, especially in relation to the Viking, as something that at once extends from cultural constructions of the male body, legitimization of male power, and normative forms of masculinity – and also always with the potential of moving beyond the automatic and naturalized connection between men and masculinity.

Methodological Considerations and Ambivalences: A Queer Reading of Masculinity

To examine the popular Viking in relation to sexuality, masculinity, and power, I make use of the method of queer reading. Developed in the 1990s, queer reading as a method emerged alongside the formation of the field of queer theory as well as with inspiration from feminist resistant readings (see Millett 1970/2012; Fetterley 1978). Early seminal works include Sedgwick's *Between Men: English Literature and Male Homosocial Desire* (1985) and *Epistemology of the Closet* (Sedgwick 1990/2008) and Alexander Doty's *Making Things Perfectly Queer: Interpreting Mass Culture* (Doty 1993). Where Sedgwick in her work destabilizes the supposed heteronormativity of Western canonical literature, Doty does the same with mass culture.

Like the feminist resistant reading, queer reading is a way of resisting or disturbing given or presupposed reading positions and choosing to approach the text from a different standpoint. What distinguishes the queer reading from a feminist reading is its premiering of sexuality and heteronormativity above sex and patriarchy (fundamental to the feminist resistant reading as it was developed in the 1970s), as well as its focus on the pluralism of the text. A queer reading does not presume to pin down the definitive meaning of a given text, but rather reads it slantwise, looks to its dissonances, silences, and ambivalences to bring forth what it *also means* (Kivilaakso, Lönngren, and Paqvalén 2012, 9–10).

As discussed above, critical and feminist readings of the popular Viking as generally interpreted makes it a problematic figure to critique and condemn. In this instance, then, understanding what the Viking also means beyond an image of normative, traditional masculinity entails not only bringing out the queer potentiality of the Viking, but also, to some extent, going against a certain critical feminist view of the possible danger inherent in this figure.

In "The Woman Batterer and the Monstrous Future of Masculinity" (2015), Lucas Gottzén asks methodological questions about how we as feminist researchers can relate to violent men and masculinities. His work concerns men who abuse women – a far cry from research on cultural representations of violent masculinities. Nonetheless, his considerations of the inevitable movement between a critical feminist condemnation of these forms of masculinities and relating and finding commonality with them, and how to handle that ambivalence (Gottzén 2015, 12), is also vital to my work. He writes that we should not "turn from violent masculinities, but rather create ways to meet with them. But the foundation of this meeting [cannot] be empathy" (ibid., 15 [my translation]).

Similar ambivalences can be found in critical queer affiliations with and considerations of masculinities. In "Loving Men", Leo Bersani explores what he calls "the erotic complicity of gay men in the very representations of masculinity that exclude us" (Bersani 1995, 116), and how gay male desire does not stand outside of "misogynous maleness" (ibid., 117). Halberstam, in "'The Killer in Me Is the Killer in You': Homosexuality and Fascism", examines the ambivalent linkages between fascism and dominant forms of masculinity and homosexuality, tracing the complex ways male homosexuality is both complicit and resistant in these discourses (Halberstam 2011). Martti Lahti similarly, in "Dressing Up in Power: Tom of Finland and Gay Male Body Politics", considers the eroticization of "white male power" (Lahti 1998, 196) in gay subcultures in relation to the complex question of the boundaries between resistance, repudiation, and reproduction.

Central to queer theory and queer readings is the idea that gender and sexuality is socially constructed and upheld, to speak with Butler, with constant repetition. However, since there is no true source of the categories of female, male, heterosexual or homosexual, these repetitions are prone to instabilities and failures. Queer researchers are interested in exactly these instabilities of normative and regulating categories of gender and sexuality.

This is the underlying theoretical framework of Mark Simpson's *Male Impersonators: Men Performing Masculinity* (1994). Here Simpson considers 1980s male-oriented culture, such as bodybuilding, action film, war film, and the buddy comedy with the impetus of pointing to the instabilities of these supposedly reassuringly masculine pursuits. He writes that his book seeks

> to emphasize the crisis of identity that faces men today in a world where 'man' and 'manly' have become freely floating signifiers with no referents – and also to *exploit* it. These essays [...] take great pleasure in celebrating the fragmentation of that which has always wished to be seen as a monolith; they have at their heart a fervent wish to denaturalize masculinity, which has in the past tried to pass itself off as unaffected, spontaneous and effortless in order to keep the mechanisms of patriarchal power secret. Homoeroticism occupies centre stage [...] because, *when revealed,* it is the greatest challenge to virility and thus masculinity's claim to authenticity, to naturalness, to coherence – to dominance. (Simpson 1994, 7 [emphases in original])

For Simpson, the latent homoeroticism of all forms of masculinity is the key to undermining dominant masculinities, in an analogue to how Waldby (1995) and Calvin Thomas (2002), respectively, understand emphasizing the sexual receptivity of the male body as key to deconstructing its dominance. Similarly, an important underlying motivation in Halberstam's *Female Masculinity* is that turning to forms of masculinity produced by bodies that are not male, white, and middle-class, makes masculinity it visible as such, and possible to understand and undermine (Halberstam 1998, 2). The homoerotic potentiality of masculinity is also central to my analysis, but my critical queer approach to masculinity extends importantly from the acknowledgment that queerness in masculinity emerges not only from (potential) male same-sex eroticism, but also from performing, finding affinity with, or embodying masculinity as female or non-male.

For Sanna Karkulehto, considering the politics of queer readings of misogynist, homosocial masculinity in Finnish literature, it is imperative to her queer reading that, as much as the texts have affected her, they and their constructions of masculinity have also been affected *by* her in some sense (Karkulehto 2012, 23). She opens her chapter with a quote from Roland Barthes – "You study what you desire or what you fear" – and a more fitting summation of queer approaches to masculinity would probably be difficult to find. What moves queer engagements with (dominant forms of) masculinity seems to be a constant tension precisely between desire and fear, between the impulse to destroy and deconstruct, and to queerly relate and recuperate.

Noble writes that "the argument that female masculinity does not notice, or is not influenced by, or does not reciprocate or return the gaze to male masculinity, cannot be supported". Rather, "the space between butches and men – male masculinity and female masculinity – [is cultivated] as vitally important spaces" (Noble 2004, xli). Locality and accountability are vital concepts to feminist knowledge production. Donna Haraway argues for the need for partial perspectives and locality as an alternative to the ideal of the "view from nowhere" purported by the supposed all-seeing, detached, and disembodied scientific, rational subject (Haraway 1988).

Following Haraway's situated perspective, for the feminist researcher, specificity, location, investments, and the view from somewhere are not complications to be jettisoned in the pursuit of pure knowledge, but rather the only possible and ethical starting points for the production of knowledge. It is from just the interstitial space between butches and men that my own investments and location in relation to this study emerge: from my own experiences of inhabiting masculinity and my enduring love for various forms of male-oriented[14] popular culture – particularly of what Yvonne Tasker (1993) would refer to as "spectacular" masculinities. My approach extends also from heeding Eve Kosofsky Sedgwick's call to "strongly resist [...] the presupposition that what women have to do with masculinity is mainly to be treated less or more oppressively by men to whom masculinity more directly pertains" (Sedgwick 1995, 13).

Halberstam writes that female masculinity has "generally been received by hetero- and homo-normative cultures as a pathological sign of misidentification and maladjustment, as a longing to be and to have a power that is always just out of reach" (Halberstam 1998, 9).[15] This has to some extent carried over to female pleasurable investments in male-oriented culture, particularly when it extends to extreme or violent forms.

Helen W. Kennedy discusses how female players of violent video games evoke concern because this form of media 'should' be antithetical to female consumers: "Very often there is an anxiety that these women are merely *playing at being like men* [...] they are ascribed a 'false consciousness' [...] suggest[ing] that these women are willing dupes in their own oppression – their pleasure is pleasure only in their own subjugation." (Kennedy 2006, 193 [my emphasis]; see also Clay 2007). Kennedy, referencing Tasker, further links a feminist failure to conceptualize women finding pleasure in violent forms of male-oriented culture as also revealing a certain snobbery towards

---

[14] Here I understand "male-oriented culture" in terms of what Lynne Pearce refers to as a given text's *"preferred reader"*, formed by the many layers of its production (Pearce 1997, 46 [emphasis in original]), pertaining to its intended reader or audience, rather than how and by whom it actually is or could be read.

[15] Like male masculinity, in other words, female masculinity is also intractably bound up with questions of power, but always also in relation to illegitimacy; (futilely) trying to lay claim to power that one is neither due nor supposed to want.

the 'low culture' form of gaming and, as in Tasker's discussion, action film (Kennedy 2006, 199).

Robert Walser, in his study on gender in the 80s heavy metal subculture, argues that there seems to be a specific empowerment to be found in this homosocial, masculine environment and music for female fans. Engagement with heavy metal enables female metal fans, in some sense, to symbolically 'lay claim' to a glorified form of patriarchal power – through a form of music that, in turn, is an attempt by working-class men to symbolically claim a patriarchal power that they as men are supposedly due, but denied as young, poor, and working class. The metal scene becomes a way through which women can positively identify with masculinity in a manner that is easily accessible, precisely because by "playing at being like men" (or, in this case, listening), they access the music in a similar way to its (intended) male audience (Walser 1993; see also Clifford-Napoleone 2015).

Here, then, methodologically cultivating the space between female and male masculinity means engaging in a reading that does not assume an oppositional[16] or alienated position in relation to cultural texts that presume male reader, but rather one of familiarity and reading pleasure. It means taking "playing at being like men" (or reading) seriously as a site of possible queerness, rather than a failure at a properly feminine, or feminist, engagement with culture. In many ways this reiterates the conflicting impulses of queer engagements with masculinity outlined above: at the same time recuperating (certain forms of) masculinity, while also challenging the straightforwardness of normative masculinity and its supposed direct linkage to men (cf Butler 1990/2006). Here the concept of queer helps elucidate not only this "vital space", as Noble calls it, but also a queer approach to the reading of the text.

Since Sedgwick's influential "Paranoid Reading and Reparative Reading, or, You're so Paranoid, You Probably Think This Introduction Is About You" (1997), queer readings have tended to be divided into two different modes: the paranoid and the reparative. This division mirrors a larger affective or post-critical turn within literary studies, criticizing the basic premise of understanding the text as hiding its meaning away beneath the surface, leaving the critic to excavate it to determine its true meaning and ideology, which has been dominant within the field since the middle of the 20th century (Björklund and Lönngren 2020).

---

[16] Judith Fetterley's foundational *The Resisting Reader: A Feminist Approach to American Fiction* (1978) understood women's reading practices in a patriarchal culture as "schizophrenic", because of forced identifications with male perspectives, and feminist readings by necessity as oppositional.

The paranoid mode has generally been understood as reading against the grain of the text, focused on tracking and revealing its hidden heteronormative assumptions or ideology. The reparative, on the other hand, has been used as an alternative strategy to read *with* the text, to place oneself *beside* the text, rather than attempt to get beneath its surface to reveal its supposed secrets. It means understanding the text's queer potentialities as something that might be obvious and ignored, rather than only hidden or repressed (see Freeman 2010; Österholm 2012; Holmqvist 2017; Manns 2018). Anu Koivunen has argued against the tendency to place the reparative mode in direct opposition to either the paranoid mode or a more general anti-social or negative impetus in queer theory (Koivunen 2010, 52; see also Weed 2012; Wiegman 2014). According to Koivunen, Sedgwick's point is not to offer the reparative reading as an alternative, but to emphasize the need for both reading strategies for queer scholarship: "Methodologically, Sedgwick offers no alternatives but suggests a political and ethical obligation to combine 'schizoid' activism and self-assurance with 'depressive' self-doubt and critical reflection" (Koivunen 2010, 59).

To some extent, the paranoid/reparative-distinction maps onto the tension in queer-theoretical approaches to masculinity outlined above – between what I've called destruction and recuperation, and between revealing masculinity as inherently unstable and even void, and the drive to reappropriate it. Or, in Sedgwick's words, the "Xray gaze of the paranoid impulse" (Sedgwick 1997, 27) versus the "additive and accreditive" desire of the reparative impulse that "wants to assemble and confer plenitude on an object that will then have resources to offer to an inchoate self" (ibid., 27–28). It is precisely this tension that has guided my reading, between the paranoid impulse to tear down and de(con)struct normative masculinity (here, of course, represented foremost by the epitomized, normative, white, supposedly straight, masculinity of the Viking), and the urge to repurpose it in some way.

A final consideration is the way white, straight masculinity has increasingly incorporated feminist, queer, and anti-racist critique in its own construction to supersede that same critique (DeAngelis 2014; Bridges and Pascoe 2014), as well as how novel narratives of crises in masculinity build from an idea of white masculinity as a victimized minority identity (Carroll 2011). Jenny Björklund and Ann-Sofie Lönngren argue that as historical context and its relation to queerness and societal acceptance change, our ways of reading must too, to consider "the power invested in different kinds of reading strategies" (Björklund and Lönngren 2020, 222).

Thus, my queer reading has not been predominantly focused on either reading forth homophobia or heteronormativity, or possible queerness, but rather precisely on where and how queerness and heteronormativity jointly construct masculinity in these texts, and the simultaneous tension and overlap between them. Grounded in my queer-theoretical approach to masculinity and my own (queer) investments in and affinities with masculinity, my queer reading serves to focus on how the masculinity of the fantasy Viking constitutes itself in terms of power, sexuality, and embodiment, and to what uses this epitomized, powerful male body can or could be put to.

Primary Material and Selection of Material

Moving on from the question of my positionality in relation to masculinity, yet another consideration is my relation to the literary material in terms of genre and fan culture. As a longtime fantasy fan, the project as a whole and the empirical selection has been guided by my pre-existing knowledge of and investments in the genre.

Popular epic fantasy, including its contemporary gritty subset, is a prolific genre, whether measuring number of works or number of pages, and my sample will by necessity be a small one of all available possible texts. In his dissertation on post-apocalyptic fiction, Andreas Nyström faces a similar problem. He finds his solution in Stephen Greenblatt's *Renaissance Self-Fashioning: From More to Shakespeare* (1980), also dealing with a large set of possible material. Greenblatt's approach is to "seize upon a handful of arresting figures who seem to contain within themselves much of what we need, who both reward intense, individual attention and promise access to larger cultural patterns" (Greenblatt 1980, 6). Greenblatt tries to find the extraordinary or "individual" that at the same time can be representative of a wider whole. His selection is in other words a strategic one, aimed at finding certain entry points into the material to extrapolate from.

Maria Margareta Österholm, studying girlhood in Swedish literature, discusses selecting material from a wide set of texts with the help of immersion and closeness. She argues for the need to understand knowledge as something that also resides in the literary text, and not only in the theory or position used to examine them (Österholm 2012, 77–78, 80–82). She grounds this understanding in the feminist tradition of situated knowledge (Haraway 1988; see further discussion above) and writes: "The picture I want to create is extensive but not at all all-encompassing – case studies, with one or two bird's eye views" (ibid., 60 [my translation]).

In other words, my selection approach is by design and necessity a subjective one, guided by my own fan investment in the genre. The empirical selection is not aimed at being randomized or universally representative, but rather at finding texts that speak to me and to each other. Following Haraway's contention that we are always implicated in some way in the research we conduct, and the importance of mapping and making use of those same investments in feminist research, I have made use of my close investments with the material and the genre; partly as a guiding principle to find and decide which texts are both individually interesting and give access to broader patterns, and partly in formulating the project – which importantly did not originate independently of the texts, but rather emerged from them. In particular Joe Abercrombie's *The First Law* has guided the formulation of the research project, in many ways also functioning as a key text in the analysis.

The empirical material consists of 18 texts, across five series and five authors (two of which write as a pair), and are as follows:

***The First Law* series (2006–2012)[17] by Joe Abercrombie**
The Blade Itself; Before They Are Hanged; Last Argument of Kings
Best Served Cold
The Heroes
Red Country

***The Shattered Sea* (2014–2015) by Joe Abercrombie**
Half a King; Half the World; Half a War

***The Iskryne Saga* (2007–2015) by Elizabeth Bear and Sarah Monette**
A Companion to Wolves; The Tempering of Men; An Apprentice to Elves

***A Land Fit for Heroes* (2008–2016) by Richard K. Morgan**
The Steel Remains; The Cold Commands; The Dark Defiles

***The Red Queen's War* (2014–2016) by Mark Lawrence**
Prince of Fools; The Liar's Key; The Wheel of Osheim

The sample includes two 'founding' texts of gritty fantasy: Abercrombie's *The First Law* and Morgan's *A Land Fit for Heroes*. Both these series enjoy a great deal of popularity and have sold many copies. Furthermore, Morgan's novels

———

[17] I have not included *The Age of Madness* (2019–2021), the latest trilogy in the *First Law* series, because it had yet to be published when this project began.

garnered considerable attention upon publication because it has a gay male protagonist.[18] Since 2008, queer representation in fantasy literature has become more common across subgenres, but then this was a rather big intervention in mainstream portrayals of masculinity in popular fantasy. I have also included Abercrombie's young adult series *The Shattered Sea* because it is at once very similar and very different to the *First Law* series – particularly when it comes to the use of the popular Viking in relation to representations of gender and power.

Mark Lawrence is a more recent gritty fantasy author, who I understand not as part of the initial gritty turn, but rather of the continuing cementing gritty fantasy as a style or trope in itself. Where Abercrombie and Morgan's work developed as a response to the post-Tolkienian fantasy, Lawrence's work, by comparison, emerged when gritty fantasy was already more or less an established part of the fantasy genre milieu. Like his predecessors, his work has enjoyed a great deal of popularity and sold well.

Much less well-known and a bit of an outlier in this selection is Elizabeth Bear and Sarah Monette's *The Iskryne Saga*. It is not explicitly labeled or discussed in terms of gritty fantasy, but like gritty fantasy it revolves around the subversion of traditional fantasy narratives in relation to masculinity, gender, and power. It is, foremost, however, an explicitly feminist and queer fantasy subversion of the popular Viking motif – I discuss this further in chapter four – and thus an interesting example to put into dialogue with the texts above.

Previous Research

The popular Viking is intimately connoted with power, might, heroics, and normative masculinity, closely tied to specific ideas of the male body, to muscularity, strength, whiteness, and unquestioned heterosexuality. Both masculinist investments in the Viking in various discourses on the 'decline' of white men and feminist/critical attempts to tear down, deconstruct, or transform this figure (Lihammer and Hesselbom 2021) ultimately hinge on the same idea of the Viking as symbolic of masculine power and might. Research on the Viking Age has also been forced to grapple with how the idea of the Viking and the Viking Age has been used and abused, particularly during the 20th century and the Nazi adoption of the Viking in their con-

---

[18] The fact that the series also has a lesbian protagonist interestingly caused almost no stir and was hardly mentioned in discussions or reviews of Morgan's work, which instead focused on the positive representation he provided of gay man through the very typically manly hero of Ringil Eskiath.

struction of Aryan purity (von Schnurbein 2016), but also today in fascist and alt-right discourses of white supremacy (Gardell 2003; Ford Burley 2019; Žiačková 2019).

In popular culture, researchers have generally focused on cultural texts, such as History Channel's *Vikings*, that is often favorably interpreted as at least complementing a focus on raids and barbarian antics with other aspects of Viking Age society (Birkett and Dale 2019; Hardwick and Lister 2019), or on areas interpreted as rife with misogynistic and racist use of the Viking, such as the contemporary metal scene (Manea 2016; Sellheim 2019; Spracklen 2020). Critical research on the popular Viking has tended to consider this motif as problematic and in need of being remedied for a number of reasons: because it has little basis in historical fact, because it represents a masculinist and/or racist construction of history, and because it presents a narrow or incomplete picture of the Viking Age.

In other words, critical engagements with the idea of the Viking have mainly focused on supplementing a skewed focus on war, invasion, and men, with overlooked parts of Viking Age history,[19] or through revealing the inherent constructed nature and instability of the concept of the Viking, as well as the national, patriarchal, and racist investments in this motif (see Sawyer 1962; Svanberg 2003; Friðriksdóttir 2021; Lihammer and Hesselbom 2021). In her reception study of Viking exhibitions, Whitehead notes that for the majority of her participants the Vikings were "heroic, adventurous warriors, excellent craftsmen and family men" (Whitehead 2014, 168), even as the general idea of the mighty Viking barbarian also lives on (ibid., 152).

However, it is not only that the historical period of the Viking Age is generally read through a raster of masculinity (whether the attempt is to reproduce this or subvert it); the Viking in itself is also powerfully symbolic of masculinity. Rather than measure the popular Viking up against historical fact, the Viking, as I see it, also relates to wider narratives on masculinities, particularly in relation to narratives on crisis masculinity. Here, then, I read the popular Viking in relation to previous research on the Viking, but also in relation to research representations of masculinity, predominately found in the fields of masculinity studies and cultural studies.

---

[19] Of course, what is considered an historically correct image of the Viking Age is also subject to change. In her work on the popular Viking, Alexandra Service gives an overview of the long-ranging debates in archeology and history that first emerged in the 1960s regarding how big a focus the Viking raider should reasonably be. The initial insistence on broadening the idea of what the Viking Age was beyond a particularly bloody and warlike society later met resistance as some researchers argued that the violent parts of Viking Age Scandinavia and its historical repercussions should not be ignored or forgotten (Service 1998, 5–7; see also Price 2020).

The idea that masculinity or men are in crisis generally emerges in mainstream discourse as something novel and acute, but it is a narrative with a long history, with veritable crises in masculinity appearing every time gender relations and society goes through major changes (Kimmel 1987; Whitehead 2002, 54–59). As discussed in the introductory paragraph, we exist in a moment of widespread fear of and concern for a perceived loss of male power and legitimacy, particularly in regard to certain groups of men. In the postindustrial West, this group predominantly consists of white men who no longer have access to traditional forms of breadwinner masculinity due to societal shifts such as changes in the labor market, the economy, and gender relations. This has sparked a sense that these men are 'losing ground' in an increasingly feminized, racialized, and queer-friendly world (Kimmel 2017). Often, this narrative as staged in terms of a 'battle of the sexes', where women are constructed as the winners in the face of men's losses, or in terms of a 'rise of minorities' at the expense of men (Carroll 2011, 4).

In feminist cultural studies and masculinity studies focused on how this moment of anxiety and perceived crisis is reflected and reproduced in media and popular culture, the idea of 'loser' masculinity or a prevailing image of loser men has been a central focus. Analyzing liquor ads in 2005, Michael Messner and Jeffrey Montez de Oca argue that these medial images construct the white man as "vulnerable":

> Caught between the excesses of a hypermasculinity that is often discredited and caricatured in popular culture and the increasing empowerment of women, people of color, and homosexuals, while simultaneously being undercut by the postindustrial economy, the 'Average Joe' is positioned as [an] ironic, vulnerable but lovable hero [...]. (Messner and Montez de Oca 2005, 1905)

These ads construct a loser man that is simultaneously threatened by women, queers, and racialized others, as well as the hypermasculinity he fails to live up to. In 2013, Kyle Green and Madison van Oort follow up on Messner and Montez de Oca's research. Analyzing the 2010 Superbowl commercials, they find that these ads construct a narrative of male victimization and failure, in particular in the areas of economic security and physical prowess. However, the 2010 images are much more aggressive in tone, expressing anger and calling men to 'take a stand' against what is portrayed as their increasing submissiveness in heterosexual relationships and precarity in the job market. Green and van Oort argue that in these ads, "the male body acts as the semiotic bedrock on which these messages about the crisis of masculinity rest", with loser men portrayed has having weak, aging, flabby, exposed bodies, sharply contrasted with idealized images of masculine hardness and vitality (Green and van Oort 2013, 714). Here, the rough, hardened body associated with working-class men proliferates; however, "the working-class man is less a sign of the working class itself than a sign of a particular masculine lifestyle", exuding strength, control, and a reassuringly solid form of masculinity (ibid., 706). Green and van Oort also place this crisis in masculinity narrative in the context of men as lifestyle consumers, where men's bodies have come increasingly into focus and masculinity itself as something one acquires and upholds through particular consumer protocols, rather than automatically embodies (Bordo 1999; Alexander 2003).

In "Powerful Women, Vulnerable Men and Postfeminist Masculinity in Men's Popular Fiction" (2014), Rosalind Gill reads men's popular fiction, so called "lad lit". She argues that what the portrayals of men in these texts have in common is that they are seen as unsuccessful losers who have failed to grow up, especially in comparison to the women in their lives, who are depicted as successful, empowered, and in full control of their lives and careers. These portrayals mock and undermine more conventional representations of male power, but this Gill understands foremost as a repudiation: "In this way an unheroic construction of masculinity might be said to represent a *postfeminist modernization of hegemonic masculinity* that allows men to hold on to social power, while presenting them as harmless and troubled victims of a world where women rule" (Gill 2014, 201 [emphasis in original]; see also Gill and Hansen-Miller 2011). Kristen Barber and Tristan Bridges look closer at hardbody masculinities in advertisements and use the term "satirical masculinity" to understand how traditional forms of masculinity are used. Satirical masculinity

> offers viewers the appearance of something progressive by seemingly mocking or deriding configurations of masculinity that have sustained feminist criticism, including hetero-romantic and hard-bodied, action hero masculinities. These images offer a playful, ironic masculinity, and invite us to take pleasure in men who clearly embody idealized forms of masculinity while engaging in 'feminine' consumption practices. But this joke really only works if the systems of power are both carefully concealed *and* reinforced. (Barber and Bridges 2017, 43 [emphasis in original])

Even as "hard-bodied, action hero masculinities" are satirized, they are still reinforced, often precisely through a focus on the physically prominent male body (Barber and Bridges 2017, 43). Key to these cultural representations of crisis or loser masculinity is that they emerge in relation to a neoliberal, postindustrial context and related socioeconomic and demographic changes. Furthermore, they revolve around anxieties precisely in the intersection between masculinity, power, and the male body, where the hardbody working-class masculine body becomes idealized and safely masculine, if not wholly safe from incorporation of feminist critique.

In *Affirmative Reaction: New Formations of White Masculinity*, Hamilton Carroll argues that white masculinity has discursively transformed itself into a minority identity in need of protection (Carroll 2011, 6). He understands white masculinity as characteristic not foremost of universality or invisibility, as it has traditionally been understood, but rather of mutability, mobility, and reaction. It retains its status by responding to social transformation, in this case by claiming injury (ibid., 10). In the cultural texts Carroll examines, white masculinity is able to retain and reiterate its hegemonic position by displacing its privilege through the incorporation of class and even queerness in its formulation. White masculinity attempts to hold on to "majority privilege" through projecting it onto "traditional sites of minority difference", such as queerness, the working class, or Irishness, and by reworking "traditional sites of masculine investment", such as the laboring body (ibid., 23). "White masculinity has, in short, learned how to manage the stakes of its own failure, thereby turning that failure into a powerful form of success", he writes (ibid., 9).

Something similar also takes place in online geek spaces, where beleaguered men use their supposed position as nerdy social outcasts to lash out against women and minorities, whom they understand to be threatening their sacred, homosocial spaces (Salter and Blodgett 2017). Beyond popular culture, Banu Gökarıksel, Christopher Neubert and Sara Smith have noted that national far-right politics in USA, Turkey and India are all based on narratives that combine the idea of virile, strongman masculinities *and* potential male victimization, "a masculinity that is simultaneously strong and weak, under constant threat and (potentially) victorious" (Gökarıksel, Neubert, and Smith 2019, 579).

Central here is that the recurring cultural narratives of the losses suffered in the West by heterosexual, white men become a powerful way of trying to recapitulate male privilege. These recapitulation attempts furthermore revolve around an idealized idea of the normative male body, tied to muscularity, strength, and bodily labor. Where this type of research has mainly focused precisely on masculine failure and loser men in media, a closer look at the popular Viking contributes a perspective on mediated crisis masculinities that take this very idealized form of masculinity into account.

Furthermore, previous research has focused on these images as aimed at and relating foremost to men, constructing a direct link between these images of male failure and real-life men. Focusing on what these media images have to say about the state of contemporary manhood, research on representations of crisis masculinity has not sufficiently taken these narratives or images into account as a wider commentary on power and embodiment – nor understood them as also possibly relevant to something beyond men.

In *Spectacular Bodies: Gender, Genre and the Action Cinema* (1993), Yvonne Tasker offers an alternate way to approach the idealized image of masculine power perpetuated by the motif of traditional, hardbody masculinity. In her book, she argues against the common understanding of the 80s Hollywood action hero as foremost a backlash against women's rights and a way to reiterate traditional forms of masculinities in the face of its supposed then-crisis (see Creed 1987; Jeffords 1994). She wants instead to "give an account, rather than an 'explanation', of both the pleasures and the political significance of these popular films" (Tasker 1993, 5).

Tasker takes the spectacular action-hero body as a complex signifier as her starting point, which she understands as "intimately bound up with class and with the operation of cultural power more generally" (ibid.). She points to the importance of understanding this spectacular display of the masculine (if not always male) muscular body as relating not only to men: "the enactment of a drama of power and powerlessness, a drama which has a special resonance for marginalised groups, is intrinsic to the anxieties of masculine identity and authority that are embodied in the figure of the struggling white hero" (ibid., 130). Here, "images of a physical power function as a counterpoint to an experience of the world as defined by restrictive limits" (ibid., 127). For Tasker, the muscular, heterosexual body of the action hero *does* relate to the felt plight of the white man's struggles. However, it is also a cultural image that effectively mobilizes discourses of powerlessness and empowerment as enacted upon the body. Thus, it becomes symbolic of a kind of general narrative of struggle that goes beyond relating only or directly to men: "If the narratives and images of the popular action cinema rarely address the specificity of particular struggles, they nevertheless powerfully dramatise the fact of struggle" (Tasker 1993, 166; see also Walkerdine 1999).

In relation to critical research on the popular Viking and discussions on masculinity and power in the current moment, I want to examine this idealized, hardbody masculinity as a complex signifier of not only masculinity but also power and powerlessness. Furthermore, it is important to be mindful of how, as Carroll writes, normative manhood has increasingly incorporated not only the discourse of marginalization (Carroll 2011), but also in various ways responded to criticism of its problematic nature (Barber and Bridges 2017). Locating my examination in the queer tension outlined in the theoretical chapter between understanding masculinity as ultimately hinging on power, legitimacy, and normativity, and as always potentially queer and possible to disrupt and appropriate for queer purposes, I seek to complicate these close linkages between Viking masculinity and power, seemingly representative only of reactionary politics or sensibilities.

Outline

This thesis consists of five chapters. Apart from this introduction, it includes three analytical chapters and a conclusion. The introduction has served to establish the aim and research questions of the study, the context, theory, method, and material, as well as previous research.

Chapter two – "Into the Fantasy North" – marks the beginning of the analysis. It gives an overview of the material and the basic worldbuilding blocks of gritty fantasy in relation to the construction of the fantasy North. The chapter opens with a reading of Mark Lawrence's *The Red Queen's War* and the close relationship between its two male protagonists: the Viking Snorri and a spoiled, vain aristocratic prince. I read this homosocial relationship in relation to the fantasy world and fantasy medievalism, and what different places and spaces come to symbolize in the fantasy landscape. Here I draw predominantly on previous critical postcolonial research on genre fantasy and worldbuilding, research on the construction of the North and the Nordics, as well as film theory on the symbolic geography of the action film working to display the muscular male body.

In chapter three – "No Future for Vikings – Temporality and Homosociality" – I continue the examination of the construction of the Viking in relation to spatiality and homosociality, but also link this to temporality. I ask what the homosocial eroticism between the Viking and other men does in these texts and how this relates to the interplay or conflict between the medieval and the modern in the material. The chapter opens with readings of journeys in and out of the North and what these come to mean in the texts, and ends with reading the male Vikings in Joe Abercrombie's *The Shattered Sea* in relation to recurring motifs of a particularly contemporary or modern form of female empowerment.

Chapter four – "The Uses and Abuses of the Viking Body" – focuses more directly on the Viking body. The defining characteristic of the Viking in this material is his muscular body, and it emerges as a site of eroticism and masculinity, as well as exploitation and anxiety. Drawing on feminist and queer action film criticism that points to the paradoxes of this form of hardbody masculinity – reassuringly masculine even as it invites (queer) objectification, simultaneously a symbol of utter empowerment and powerlessness, glorifying the muscular body even as it also plays on the fear of being reduced to the body – I examine the Viking as an object in these texts. Here I focus on the threat of homoeroticism and the queer gaze in Abercrombie's *Best Served Cold* and the utilization of the Viking body for feminist purposes in Elizabeth Bear and Sarah Monette's *The Iskryne Saga.*

The final chapter – "Steel as the Answer?" – summarizes the analytical discussions of the previous chapters and makes some concluding remarks about the popular Viking.

Chapter 2: Into the Fantasy North

Finding the map is the first step in entering the fantasy world, according to Dianna Wynne Jones (Jones 2006, x). The importance of worldbuilding and landscape in the fantasy text is well-established (Mendlesohn 2008; Ekman 2013; Ekman and Taylor 2016; Roine 2016), as is the close connection between character and landscape (Balfe 2004; Langer 2008). Understanding the fantasy text, and the use of the Viking motif, means attending to how the Viking characters emerge in relation to landscape and place. This chapter examines the Viking motif in conjunction to the fantasy text, landscape, and worldbuilding, and furthermore puts it in relation to spatiality and power. The chapter also introduces and gives an overview of the material.

Mark Lawrence's *Prince of Fools* (*The Red Queen's War* #1) opens with the eponymous prince Jalan being called by the queen, his grandmother, to attend a series of prisoner interviews. Jalan is in a foul mood as he steps into the heart of his grandmother's imperial power: "I've never liked the throne room. Not for the arching grandness of it, or the history set in grim-faced stone and staring at us from every wall, but because the place has no escape routes. Guards, guards, and more guards, along with the scrutiny of that awful old woman who claims to be my grandmother" (Lawrence 2015a, 13).

Jalan, self-described as a "coward", is immediately introduced to the reader as a failure of a man: a disappointment to his family and an irresponsible young man who spends his days drinking, gambling, and womanizing. His place in the succession has been usurped by his cousin Serah, who instead is described as a feisty, capable young woman, "better suited to the hunt than to court". She "contain[s] not one ounce of whatever it is that makes a princess" but has "a vicious right hook and a knack for kicking the tenderest spot that a man owns" – which Jalan knows well due to his untoward advances (ibid.). Jalan, in other words, almost immediately comes to encapsulate a form of loser masculinity, where he is not only consistently failing in most areas in life, but also portrayed as inferior particularly in relation to his female relatives, depicted as strong and accomplished women (cf Gill 2014).

Where the introduction of Jalan focus on his many failings as a man and a prince, the trilogy's other main character, the Viking warrior Snorri ver

Snagason, is presented in quite a different manner. Sold into slavery by an enemy, Snorri has been bought by the queen of the Red March and is led into the throne room in chains, introduced through Jalan's point of view:

> The prisoner strode into the throne room with his head held high. He dwarfed the four guards around him. I've seen taller men, though not often. I've seen men more heavily muscled, but seldom. I've even on rare occasions seen men larger in both dimensions, but this Norseman carried himself like a true warrior. [...] He walked in like murder, and when they jerked him to a halt before the chamberlain he snarled. *Snarled.* I could almost count the gold crowns spilling into my hands when I got this one to the pits! (Lawrence 2015a, 24 [emphasis in original])

Snorri is not the first prisoner to be paraded through the throne room: he has been preceded by a "Nuban warrior", a "corsair", and a "Slav" (Lawrence 2015a, 22–23). Jalan dismisses all of them as clumsy, slow, or generally unimpressive, all the while daydreaming about his female lovers. Snorri, however, captures his attention, thanks to his might and muscularity, as well as the economic gain Jalan hopes to make from his Viking brawn. Jalan has large gambling debts, which he plans to win back by forcing the enslaved Snorri to fight in the city's gladiatorial pits.

As Snorri speaks of his northern home, Jalan, despite his cowardice, is so enthralled he's suddenly seduced by visions of adventures in the North: "[...] damned if I didn't want to be a Viking too, swinging my axe on a longboat sailing up the Uulisk Fjord, with the spring ice crunching beneath its hull. Every time he paused for breath the foolishness left me and I counted myself very lucky to be warm and safe in Red March [...]" (Lawrence 2015a, 26).

The opening of *Prince of Fools* immediately brings into view many of the elements central to the fantasy Viking, and to the analysis here: the importance of world and place in the text and in relation to characters; the Viking as defined and characterized by the body; hierarchal homosociality and comparison between different masculinities and their relation to questions of power, gender, and women; as well as the contrast between the Viking and his cold Northern home and the rest of the fantasy world.

In research on the popular Viking in historical fiction, TV and film, these Viking tales generally revolve around highlights, or areas, of popular interest in regard to the Viking Age – primarily Viking raids and conquest – but also a more general chronology of Viking Age history (Service 1998; Harty 2011; Bennett and Wilkins 2019; Birkett and Dale 2019; Hardwick and Lister 2019). Here, importantly, the epic and gritty fantasy differs. Fantasy Vikings, as we will see, do battle (a lot) and occasionally also raid, but unlike most other mass medial envisioning of Vikings, the Viking characters do not 'act out' periods of Viking Age history. Instead, the significance of the Viking – and, by extension, the North – in the fantasy text emerges in relation foremost to worldbuilding. How the fantasy Viking and the fantasy North figure in the worldbuilding of gritty fantasy is the guiding question of this chapter.

Fantasy Cartography

The construction of the world is central to speculative fiction, and particularly to fantasy literature (Mendlesohn 2008; Ekman 2013; Ekman and Taylor 2016; Roine 2016). This is perhaps most clearly exemplified by the predominance of the fantasy map, typically placed first in the fantasy text. In this way, the map functions as the reader's first introduction to the fantasy world. Stefan Ekman understands the fantasy map as not only descriptive, but an instrumental part in the construction of the imaginary geography of the fantasy land (Ekman 2013, 20). The fantasy map, furthermore, is part of both the construction of a believable fantasy world and a guide to the plot – only places central to the story and the narrative will show up on it (Ekman 2013; see also Jones 2006, xi).

Fantasy maps and fantasy worldbuilding both tend to be neo-medievalist in style, meaning that the maps are designed to come across as pseudo-archaic (Ekman 2013, 25, 41) and adhere roughly to a European medieval understanding of the world, with a geography centered largely on the northern hemisphere (ibid., 29). Ekman writes: "This is a map whose subject is not a non-specific 'west' but a number of regions defined as 'the West', a cultural, political, and historical as well as geographical location [...]" (Ekman 2013, 55). Helen Young, in *Race and Popular Fantasy Literature: Habits of Whiteness* (2016), describes the quintessential fantasy world: "[it] does not resemble a map of modern Europe, but it does locate the action in the corresponding part of the globe: there is a great sea to the west, icy wastes to the north, and hotter, dryer lands to the south" (Young 2016, 29). Carolyne Larrington, describing the world of *Game of Thrones*, makes a similar observation:

> Like Tolkien's Middle Earth, *Game of Thrones/A Song of Ice and Fire* constructs its fantasy out of familiar building blocks [...] These blocks are chiselled out of the historical and imaginary medieval past, out of the medieval north, with its icy wastes, its monsters and its wolves; out of the medieval west, with its recognisable social institutions of chivalry, kingship,

its conventions of inheritance and masculinity; out of the medieval Mediterranean, with its hotchpotch of trading ports, pirates, slavers and ancient civilisations; and out of the medieval fantasies of the exotic east, where Mongol horsemen harried fabled cities of unimaginable riches, and where bizarre customs held sway among strange tribes on the edges of the known world – and even beyond. (Larrington 2015, 16)

Popular fantasy's preoccupation with the European Middle Ages has long been understood as a heritage from the influence of J.R.R. Tolkien, a medievalist scholar, that has, over time, become a genre convention that is not only shaped by popular medievalism, but also, in part, reproduces it (Young 2016). Katheryn Hume, writing on medievalism in fantastical literature, argues that this fantastic medievalism exists on a spectrum that stretches from an attempt at historical faithfulness to more or less evoking a feeling of the medieval through the use of, for example, kings, swords, knights, and castles (Hume 2004). Young and Kavita Mudan Finn further remind us that "[t]he Eurocentric conventions of medievalist fantasy connect imagined worlds not with realities of any historical Middle Ages, but with centuries of spatial and temporal medievalist storytelling" (Young and Mudan Finn 2022, 11).

Postcolonial research on fantasy worldbuilding and geography has moreover considered fantasy medievalism in terms of a Western imperialist construction of geography, time, and history (Balfe 2004; Langer 2008; Young 2016). For Myles Balfe, the generic, medievalist fantasy landscape is inherently moralistic, with the West as the center of the world in a literal, plot-related, political, and moral sense. The centrality of the medieval West in fantasy furthermore reflects and reproduces familiar and long-standing Western constructions of the Orient as Other and inferior (Balfe 2004). Where Balfe is concerned with fantasy orientalism, Young considers whiteness to be intrinsic to not only the fantasy world, but also to the development of popular fantasy as a genre. She writes:

> Fantasy habitually constructs the Self through Whiteness and Otherness through an array of racist stereotypes, particularly but not exclusively those associated with Blackness. The Middle Ages are, anachronistically, considered White space in the popular imagination [...] The imagined worlds are dominated by Whiteness, imagined as a (never-extant) pre-race utopia [...]. (Young 2016, 11–12; see also Loponen 2019)

For Young and Balfe, popular fantasy literature is formed in large part by European imperialism: through its taproot texts, a Eurocentric formulation of history, and the privileging of whiteness, what Larrington describes as the "medieval West" becomes the moral heart of the fantasy text, with the non-white and the non-Western emerging as Other.

According to Balfe, this geographical–narrative demarcation between center and margin in the fantasy text mirrors the moral demarcation between good and evil so central to the post-Tolkienian fantasy[20] (Balfe 2004). Jessica Langer, examining Eurocentrism in multiplayer fantasy game *World of Warcraft*, argues instead that while the world of the game builds on an existing First World–Third World geographical–moral dichotomy, the difference here is not derived from a clear-cut dichotomy of good versus evil. Rather it is drawn "between familiarity and otherness [...] civilized and savage, self and other, and center and periphery" (Langer 2008, 87).

Foundational to postcolonial theory is the understanding of Western imperialism and (post)coloniality as producing a discursive knowledge regime that positions the West as the spatial and temporal center and epitome of the world and of history, in turn constructing the rest of the world as provincial and 'lagging behind' Western modernity. Walter D. Mignolo and Madina V. Tlostanova understand this construction of the world as formulated precisely in relation to the Western notion of the medieval:

> The point of reference of modernity is the European Renaissance founded, as an idea and interpretation of a historical present, on two complementary moves: the colonization of time and the invention of the Middle Ages, and the colonization of space and the invention of America that became integrated into a Christian tripartite geo-political order: Asia, Africa and Europe. The world map drawn by Gerardus Mercator and Johannes Ortelius worked together with theology to create a zero point of observation and of knowledge: a perspective that denied all other perspectives. (Tlostanova and Mignolo 2006, 205–206)

Postcolonial theory points to how this construction of the world and its history creates a landscape of power, where the ostensibly unmarked West becomes the natural and given center of the world. To some extent, this is literalized (cf Roine 2016) in the medievalist fantasy world. Where Balfe and Young place the fantasy text and world within a larger context of Western imperialism and trace the literary-historical influences of this construction of

---

[20] See introduction.

the fantasy world and the text, Langer points to this colonial relationality of familiarity and otherness, center and periphery, as a function of the worldbuilding itself, not just the literary-historical influences on the genre's development. This means understanding the medieval fantasy world as a landscape formed by, and to some extent literalizing, discourses of power in its worldbuilding.

The maps[21] in my material also reflect and reproduce this standardized medievalist fantasy geography outlined above, with few variations. Of the maps, only *The Iskryne Saga* one does not portray a larger part of the fantasy world, focusing only on the North itself. However, the map is titled "The North of the World", evidently putting it in relation to a wider fantasy world. The rest of the maps in the material display three central regions: put in Larrington's terms, the "icy wastes" to the North, the "medieval west" in the middle, and "hotter, dryer lands" at the bottom (Larrington 2015, 16). The North on these maps is marked as a remote space, separated from the center of the maps by both distance and geographical features, such as forests, mountains, or ice.

On Lawrence's map, the Northern territory is separated from the mainland by a "Devouring Sea" and placed right beneath the "Bitter Ice". On the Iskryne map, scant Northern settlements are located between a big mountain range and "Wilderlands & Ice. Here be Wyverns & Trolls". On Abercrombie's and Morgan's maps, the mountains grow in both number and height the closer they get to the Northern edge of the map, marking the space beyond as harsher and wilder. These areas are sparsely populated, with only a few larger settlements, and instead are filled with trees and mountains, features that according to Ekman signal wilderness (Ekman 2013, 35), in direct contrast to the flat, settled, agricultural land of the medieval West. The fantasy North is not only placed at the edge of the map, but also on the outskirts of human territory, effectively constructing the North as the upper – and outer – edge of the fantasy world (cf Marques 2016).

The map of the *First Law* novels is a particularly salient example; it is construed as a circle, with "the Union", its main (both narratively and structurally within the world) medieval West placed right in the middle of

---

[21] All texts in the material are accompanied by maps. As a rule, there is one map per series – with the exception of *The Shattered Sea*, where the map grows in scope with every instalment, which mirrors the plot and the movement of the characters across the world. Abercrombie's *The Heroes* also includes a separate map, but it depicts a single valley where a major battle takes place. Since it portrays such a minor part of the world, I have not taken this one into account because here I am interested in the overarching relationality of the fantasy world.

the map, effectively marking the rest of the world as its periphery. To the south is the state of Styria, a corrupt dukedom concerned only with riches and treachery, and the empire of Gurkhul, a desert realm of slavery, religious extremism, and cannibalism, reiterating a similar oriental construction of the fantasy world to that outlined by Balfe (Balfe 2004).

In these texts, the relationality of the fantasy land is reflected in the plot, with the relations between the North, the West, and the South marked by conflict. In *The First Law*, the North goes to war against the Union to reclaim land the Union has long since annexed, setting off a conflict that lasts over the course of the entire (as of yet, unfinished) series, at the same time as Gurkhul attacks the Union from the south. In *The Iskryne Saga*, the North is similarly invaded by an enemy nation, inspired by the Roman Empire, attempting to annex and civilize it.

In *A Land Fit for Heroes*, the North is destabilized by the orientalist Yhelteth Empire,[22] in an attempt to seize control. While the main conflict in *The Shattered Sea* is between warring factions of the North itself, one of the main causes for the strife is the new religion of the "One God" coming from outside to try to convert the region. Furthermore, a large section of the plot revolves around the North coming into contact with civilization.

In *The Red Queen's War*, the main conflicts relating to the North are internal, but they threaten to release cataclysmic horrors hiding in the icy wilderness that would spell doom for the entire fantasy world. The recurring relationality of the North and the West (and, to a lesser extent, the North and the South) are then constructed in terms of a barbarian–civilization dichotomy, where the North with its "icy wastes […] monsters and […] wolves" emerges in direct contrast to "the medieval west with its […] institutions of chivalry, kingship, […] conventions of inheritance and masculinity" (Larrington 2015, 16).

These geographical demarcations we can see reflected in the above introduction of Snorri, snarling in the throne room. The fantasy Viking emerges in close alignment with the Nordic landscape, building on the idea of the North and the Nordic as shaped by an "idealization of the man of the hinterlands and the harsh conditions under which he lived" (Klinge 1984, 260; see also Schram 2009; Loftsdóttir, Kjartansdóttir, and Lund 2017). Furthermore,

---

[22] As far as conflict goes, Morgan's text differs slightly from the rest; while the basic relationality of the worldbuilding is very similar, the 'unmarked' Western territory, called Trelayne, does not function as the sole center of the world, but so also does the southern, orientalist empire of Yhelteth. Trelayne and Yhelteth are allied, and their respective relations to the North remain largely the same as in the other texts.

this connects to a wider cultural motif of the North as an arena of and for wilderness and adventure. Peter Davidson, researching the idea of the North as a literary motif, writes:

> To say 'we leave for the north tonight' brings immediate thoughts of a harder place, a place of dearth: uplands, adverse weather, remoteness from cities. A voluntary northward journey implies a willingness to encounter the intractable elements of climate, topography and humanity. In an English-language fiction, the words 'we leave for the north tonight' would probably be spoken in a thriller, a fiction of action, of travel, of pursuit over wild country. (Davidson 2005, 11)

Indeed, the construction of the North as wild, barbarous and other to civilization is one with a long history, dating back to Antiquity. In *Southern Perspectives on the North: Legends, Stereotypes, Images and Models* (2001), Peter Stadius presents an overview of historical constructions of the North. During Antiquity, the North, constituting everything beyond the Roman Empire, was considered a wild and dangerous periphery. At the same time, the North was also understood in terms of utopia, an Arcadia of wonders and freedom. According to Stadius, while these twinned conceptualizations of the North – as at once barbaric and utopian – have persisted for centuries, the geographic landscape they are understood to encapsulate has shifted with time.[23]

During the Enlightenment, the idea of the North became increasingly associated with modernity and progress, which has continued into contemporary times, where the North, or the Nordics, is generally associated with social progress, the welfare state, and (gender) equality. Even so, these ideas have not erased previous conceptualizations of the North. They exist side by side, constructing the North from "a mixture of older images of a barbarian and brutal periphery, and later images of the North as the home of progress and modernity" (Stadius 2001, 25).

Next to, and entwined with, these historical constructions of the savage alterity of the North, runs a long-standing conceptualization of the North as marked by closeness and familiarity in the Anglo-American imagination. In

---

[23] Not unlike the Viking, the concepts of *the Nordics* and *the North* are fluid and historically contingent. Davidson argues that what is considered 'the North' is, by necessity, always relational and therefore open to change (Davidson 2005, 9). The North of Europe, which the idea of the Nordic developed from, has shifted over time and place, and used to include not only the Nordic countries of today, but also the Baltic region, Germany, Poland, Russia, and Scotland (Stadius 2001, 5; Jalava and Stråth 2017, 36).

Popular Vikings: Constructions of Viking Identity in Twentieth Century Britain (1998), Alexandra Service understands the Viking as a barbarian motif, and writes on the generally positive portrayal of the Viking barbarian in British media: "The difference may simply be one of degrees of foreignness: Huns, Mongols and the Tartars are inescapably the Other to Western perceptions, whereas Vikings, though perhaps admittedly barbarous, are *our* barbarians" (Service 1998, 147 [emphasis in original]).

While the construction of the Viking as barbarian originated from Viking Age raids on British shores, Britain has a to a large extent incorporated Vikings into its own national history. The historical connections between Viking Age Scandinavia and what is today the UK are many and seem to have consisted of trade and settlements as much as raids and battles. However, the idea of Britain's 'Viking past' also remains a part of its people's own self-image: for example, this idea played a significant role in 19th century colonial constructions of Britain as a far-reaching, expansionist people (Newby 2013).

North America's historical links to a Viking past is much more tenuous, but that has not stopped people from attempting to construct such a history. The discovery of Vinland by Leif Eriksson and his sons as described in *The Saga of the Greenlanders* and *The Saga of Erik the Red*, written down between 1220 and 1280, has occasionally been interpreted as an alternative origin story for the United States, predating Christopher Columbus' arrival on the continent. Despite the fact that there is no historical evidence for any continuity between the events described in the fictional sagas and the founding of the United States, this has historically been an important political 'alternative' to the origin story of the United States in some places (Kolodny 2012). Today the interest in the idea of a North American Viking past is mainly tied to white nationalism and attempts to create a "pseudo-history of white superiority", as Robert Ford Burley puts it (Ford Burley 2019, 208).

Following this, we can understand the relational 'othering' of the fantasy North as different to the oriental and colonial constructions of the East and South described by Balfe and Langer – not to mention in comparison to the constructions of the South in my material. This can be seen by the comparison between the warrior prisoners paraded before the throne – "Nuban warrior", a "corsair", and a "Slav", all connotated with barbarianism, as well as racialization – and Snorri, whose Northern Viking masculinity is described as foremost among them and he as being the only one to catch Jalan's interest.

Young understands the construction and motif of the utopian–barbarian North as part of the fantasy genre's Eurocentrism and incessant attachment to whiteness (Young 2016, 26–28). Tracing the popularity of the Northman figure in fantasy literature to Robert E. Howard's *Conan the Barbarian*, she writes: "His 'dual identity of being a savage, but being white', makes him naturally suited to lead the softer, more decadent and corrupted peoples of the south [...] Conan is the Germanic barbarian tribesman of Tacitus, filtered through nineteenth-century American Anglo-Saxonism and re-modeled for twentieth-century consumption" (Young 2016, 26). Following Young, then, we can understand the ambivalent familiarity of the North as intimately connected to whiteness.

As critical whiteness scholars have pointed out, Nordic whiteness has a long history of being considered the epitome of whiteness. In their introduction to an issue of *Scandinavian Studies* on Nordic whiteness, Catrin Lundström and Benjamin R. Teitelbaum write:

> To be white is to be Nordic; to be Nordic is to be white. These are associations centuries in the making. Nordics have long functioned as whiteness standard bearers in pseudoscientific race typologies [...] This special issue seeks to examine Nordic whiteness as a fluid and contested but also an enduring and powerful phenomenon, one that continues to shape global politics, culture, and social relations (Lundström and Teitelbaum 2017, 151; see also Loftsdóttir and Jensen 2012).

Kristín Loftsdóttir, studying Icelandic nation branding, argues that modern-day Iceland encapsulates many of the particularities of Nordic exoticism. Through discourses on the distant mystical North and the wildness of its landscape, "the North has become particularly desirable because it retains its characteristics as unexplored, strange and wild, while some of its parts remain more easily removed from histories of colonization and racism than many other parts of the world [...]" (Loftsdóttir 2015, 257). According to Loftsdóttir, the wildness of the North becomes evocative in this way because it can emerge as other to civilization, seemingly without the baggage of colonialism that shapes similar constructions of many other places. Thus, the North represents, supposedly, an ideological 'safe' otherness – as well as one that shares the supposed familiarity of whiteness. Loftsdóttir further describes this in terms of the good and bad duality of the savage, reading the Northern wilderness as "an 'Eden before the fall' where the exotic can be explored without any critical perspectives of unequal power relationships in the world" (Loftsdóttir 2015, 257).

Following Langer's understanding of the fantasy world as mediated through dichotomies of self and other, center and margin, civilized and barbarian on the level of worldbuilding, I suggest that the fantasy North becomes meaningful in these texts as the barbarian Other to the civilized center, foremost the medieval West. Importantly, however, this demarcation does not primarily hinge upon difference. Constructions of the wild, utopian, and pure North have long been part of not just European identity formation, but also colonial narratives of Western hegemony and racist narratives about white superiority. The otherness of the fantasy North, then, is one built from the familiarity of whiteness where the barbarian–civilization dichotomy can be made meaningful, supposedly without recourse to questions of power. In the fantasy text, the North can function as a land of remote wilderness untroubled by questions of colonial difference.

The Fantasy North and the Fantasy of the North

In "Moving Beyond Tolkien's Medievalism", George B. Elliot criticizes critical attempts to all-too-easily fit popular fantasy into the medievalist mold set by Tolkien, regardless of whether the text actually supports it. He takes the figure of the Viking as his prime example: "That the mention of a raiding island culture in a fantasy series immediately brings to mind conventional depictions of Vikings [...] bespeaks a decidedly Northern and Western European-centric bias inculcated into the expectations of the general fantasy readership", he writes (Elliot 2015, 184).

Elliot raises a fair contention: popular fantasy and critical attention to it is certainly marked by a "Northern and Western-European-centric bias". Furthermore, while popular fantasy is and has for a long time been dominated by Anglophone texts and perspectives,[24] since the construction of a fantastic secondary world is so central to much popular fantasy, it continuously reworks and variates its medievalist content and creates its fantasy Norths from a number of sources – even if much of the general underlying blueprint often remains the same. Just as in Hume's discussion of fantastical medievalism, the presence of Vikings and the Nordic in these texts exists on a spectrum of changing levels of attention to historical detail and specificity.

In the preface to *A Companion to Wolves* (*The Iskryne Saga* #1), Elizabeth Bear and Sarah Monette note that

> [t]he world of Iskryne is not Earth, but certain of its human cultures are not unlike certain historical Terran cultures. We have chosen to recognize this

---

[24] As Kim Wilkins has discussed in regard to the Australian fantasy market, fantasy literature tends to be dominated by "European landscapes, history, and storytelling traditions [...]" even when produced elsewhere in the world (Wilkins 2011, 133).

> kinship by rendering the language of the people in this story in a melange of Norse, Anglo-Saxon, and other Germanic languages [...] in the hopes that this alien familiarity and familiar alienness will help readers as they enter into this cold and perilous world. (Bear and Monette 2007, ix)

Bear and Monette point to the historical inspirations for their work, as well as the importance of understanding this as reworked within in the context of the construction of the fantasy world. Furthermore, the amalgamation of Norse, Anglo-Saxon, and Germanic peoples into a generalized Northman is a long-standing figure of thought (Eilertsen 2012), with a long history also in fantasy literature (Lönnroth 2017, 165).

This is reflected in my material: while Lawrence refers to his Northern inhabitants as "Vikings", and there are "Norse" and "Norsemen" in Bear and Monette's work, they are in Abercrombie's *First Law* simply referred to as "Northmen". In Morgan's texts, the inhabitants of the North are styled "Majaks",[25] and are tribal and horse-bound, sharing many similarities with Tolkien's Rohan, an amalgamation of Norse, Germanic, and Anglo-Saxon imagery (Lönnroth 2017, 165). Much of their gods and culture is inspired by Norse mythology, but they are also described as a nomadic steppe people, perhaps drawing inspiration from Mongol history.

In *The Red Queen's War* and *The Shattered Sea*, the North is presented as a direct analogue to the present-day Nordics: these texts take place not directly in an imaginary past, but in the far future. Through an unspecified apocalyptic event these worlds have (re)turned to some version of the Middle Ages or the Viking Age, and the North in these texts is something akin to a 'new' version of Viking Age Scandinavia that has replaced the contemporary Nordics. The fantasy Norths of the rest of the texts are more generalized, drawing inspiration from a wider idea of the Old North than only Viking Age Scandinavia, which I interpret as the same Norse, Germanic, Anglo-Saxon "melange" described by Bear and Monette.

That said, my purpose here, to return to Elliot, is not to close down alternate readings or state that these constructions of the fantasy North definitely represent an analogue to the Nordics and nothing else. The general, popular idea of the Viking and the Old North are complex and myriad constructs that do not represent one historical truth of Viking Age Scan-

---

[25] A word of Slavic origin, and the name of a nunatak (a type of mountain) in Antarctica. According to the Oxford Polish-English Dictionary, "majak" means "phantom". Moreover, "Mayak" refers to a Russian site for the handling of biohazard waste. However, the Majak goddess of blood and vengeance in Morgan's series is named Kelgris ("cuddle pig" in Swedish) in the first novel – altered to Kwelgrish in subsequent installments – so it is uncertain how intentional these references actually are.

dinavia or other parts of Nordic history. Rather, it is a construction drawn from a wide array of images and ideas about a generalized and fictitious North or the Nordics, many of them inspired by popular culture, rather than historical fact.

Importantly, the field of Nordic studies also emphasizes the constructed nature of the idea of Norden or the Nordics as a unified region (Stråth and Sørensen 1997), critically examining the supposed or automatic affinity of the Nordic countries and pointing to their divergent histories and formations (Kettunen 1999; Christiansen and Petersen 2001; Jalava and Stråth 2017); the strategic use of the idea of a united Norden in international politics (Götz 2009); and the increasing use of 'Nordic' as a brand, in both nation branding and for commercial purposes (Browning 2007; Strang, Marjanen, and Hilson 2020; Angell and Larsen 2022). Critical attention has also been paid to how the Nordics may become naturalized as an imagined community within academia, as a way of delineating and constructing research communities and knowledge production in relation to geopolitics and questions of difference (Dahl, Liljeström, and Manns 2016). When I discuss the fiction and fluidity of the fantasy North, it is not as a failure to depict, or in relation to, a real-world, pre-existing Nordics, but rather to point to the specificity of how fantasy literature incorporates and builds from the flux of ideas of the Nordics and the North.

In many ways, the material is a continuation of the inherent instability and flux of these images and ideas. That said, I am here not mainly interested in whether or not these fantasy Norths are 'supposed' to represent any historical time period or place – I read them as foremost congruent with ideas about the Nordics, the North, and Viking Age Scandinavia in order to understand their *function* within the texts.

Above, I demonstrated how the consistent characteristic of the fantasy North is as the wild, cold, barbarian margin of the fantasy world, particularly in relation to the pseudo-medieval West, and how this peripherality hinges upon a narrative of simultaneous familiarity and otherness threaded through a colonial construction of the commonality of whiteness. This, I argue, is key to understanding the fantasy North in the fantasy text and worldbuilding: its relationality and function, which, while shaped and implicated by historical constructions of these regions, is not necessarily reducible to it. The same goes for the fantasy Viking, which I read as such not only based on the term 'Viking' or the historical facts that seems to have inspired it – which vary across the texts – but rather precisely its function and characteristics as it relates to the fantasy world.

"A life of violence and savagery": The Fantasy Viking

Characteristic for genre fantasy is not only the world, but also the direct relationship between characters and landscape. Fantasy characters "are generally defined by their deeds and exist in a dialectic relationship with 'their' landscapes, embodying the core values that the landscape is thought to represent" (Balfe 2004, 77). In *The Tough Guide to Fantasyland*, fantasy author Diana Wynne Jones's mock encyclopedia detailing common fantasy tropes, "Barbary Vikings" and "Northern barbarians" both make an appearance. They are defined as large, muscular, and violent warriors and barbarians, often scantily clad despite the cold climate. According to Jones, they are portrayed as largely and overwhelmingly masculine, and their societies are generally male-dominated and homosocial. They can function as either villains or heroes but tend to hold the role of fighter and berserker in the fantasy text (Jones 2006, 15, 135).

Jones' satiric definitions of what I call the fantasy Viking holds mostly true for my material, too. The fantasy North is a violent and warlike place, and its (male) inhabitants and most prominent Viking/Northman characters in the texts are warriors – that is, their defining traits seem to be their skills in battle, their ferociousness, and ability to use and withstand violence. Exceptions do exist, but they generally prove the rule, such as Yarvi and Skara in *The Shattered Sea*, whose development revolves around the fact that they are not warriors in a society that value violence and physical strength above all. Another example is Calder in *The Heroes* (*The First Law* #5), who is driven by the difficulty of being a Northman with more brains than brawn (discussed further in chapter three). For the rest, most characters adhere to the general outline set by Snorri, discussed in the beginning of this chapter, and to Jones' definition.

In *A Companion to Wolves* (*The Iskryne Saga* #1), the reader is introduced as early as the second page to the wolfcarls, an elite warrior band bonded to giant wolves who fight trolls:

> The wolfcarl was a big man, almost as tall and stocky as a troll himself, wild-bearded, his graying red hair braided back from his temples; the edge of the axe he carried was bright with nicks and sharpening. He was Hrolleif, the Old Wolf, high-ranked in the wolfthreat, and Njall knew the villagers – and the manor – owed him obedience and fear. (Bear and Monette 2007, 2)

A similar scene to the introductions of both Hrolleif and Snorri can be found in *The Blade Itself* (*The First Law* #1). Envoys have unexpectedly arrived from the North and attend a meeting of the King's council: "One was a grizzled old warrior with a scar and a blind eye [...] The other was cloaked and hooded, every feature hidden, and so big he made the whole hall seem out of proportion. The benches, the tables, even the guards, all suddenly looked like small versions designed for children" (Abercrombie 2006, 131).

Here, the Northmen emerge in contrast to the lords gathered in the room, described as dressed in gold, jewels, and finery, and especially to the old and ill Union King "lolling like a great hill swathed in fur and red silk, head squashed into his shoulders by the weight of the great, sparkling crown" (Abercrombie 2006, 130). As in the other two examples, there is here a great emphasis on space and place, with the great Viking body, scarred, muscular, and marked by violence and use, juxtaposed to the opulence and hierarchal power of the throne room, the manor, and the royal council chamber.

These are not isolated descriptions, but recur throughout the texts, such as when a Union nobleman lays eyes on Northman Logen Ninefingers and is appalled by this barbarian visage (a section which has here been significantly cut down):

> Never in his life had Jezal seen a more brutish-looking man. [...] His whole face, in fact, was slightly beaten, broken, lop-sided, like that of a prize fighter who has fought a few bouts too many. [...] He wore a long fur cloak, and a leather tunic set with gold, but this height of barbaric splendor only made him look more savage, and there was no missing the long, heavy sword at his belt. The Northman scratched at a big pink scar through the stubble on his cheek [...] and Jezal noticed one of his fingers was missing. As though any further evidence of a life of violence and savagery was necessary. (Abercrombie 2006, 265)

The Steel Remains (*A Land Fit for Heroes* #1), on the other hand, seemingly attempts to subvert these recurring descriptions of barbarous Northmen stomping into civilized halls and terrifying the nobles. When we are introduced to the Northman protagonist Egar Dragonbane, it is as he is musing on his youth back when he left the North for adventures in the South:

> He believed implicitly what his fathers and brothers told him, and what they told him was, basically, that the Majak were the roughest toughest drinkers and fighters on Earth, that of all the Majak clans, the Skaranak were the hardiest, and that the northern grasslands were the only place any real man would ever consider living.

> It was a philosophy that Egar disproved for himself, at least in part, one night in a tavern in Ishlin-ichan a few years later. (Morgan 2008, 11)

In a Southern tavern, the young Egar gets drunk and picks a fight with a professional soldier. He gets his ass kicked and his pride wounded, and the older Egar notes how the incident schooled him on his prejudices about *"effete fucking southerners"* (Morgan 2008, 12 [emphasis in original]). Apparently, however, he proved himself well enough that the soldier offered him work as a mercenary (ibid., 13).

Moreover, while Morgan initially seems to attempt to complicate the image of the Northman, Egar eventually does get a proper Viking description when he is later described as

> a figure from legend emerging out of battlefield mist. Broad and tall and tangled looking, hair a wild knotted mess with little iron talismanic ornaments hanging from it. One leather-sheathed blade of his staff lance jutted up over his shoulder, there was a short-handled axe matched with a broad-bladed dirk at his belt. He smelled of marsh and cold [...] (Morgan 2008, 292)

If we recall the relationality of the fantasy map – of the wild North in relation to the medieval West – the Viking character here performs a similar function. Reflecting the characteristics of the cold, wild North, the Viking character emerges as other to civilization – which is made symbolic here through references to the monarchy and aristocracy: throne rooms, advisory councils, and manors, bloodlines and questions of succession, queens, princes, and nobility. What all these descriptions come back to, furthermore, is the body. Muscular, tall, large, armed, scarred, bearded, brutish-looking – the Viking is established as such mainly through his spectacularly masculine body.

The term 'Viking' "instantaneously evokes an image of bloodthirsty warriors, weapons, hoards, burning monasteries and heroic battles", writes Gudrun Whitehead (2014, 2). Service further understands the Viking as "a creature of extremes [...] A Viking, it seems, cannot be simply ordinary. Vikings must be intense in some way; they must be the tallest and the strongest and the blondest, [...] and must bare their muscular limbs in the skimpiest of outfits, undaunted by the icy Northern winds" (Service 1998, 64). The Viking, in other words, is a motif long associated with extreme masculinity.

In the fantasy text, the Viking is clearly defined by his extreme bodily comportment and masculinity in relation precisely to the luxury, excesses, and power of civilization. We can see this for example in the scene from *The*

First Law above, where the "grizzled" visage of the Northman warrior is directly contrasted to the sleeping Union King, clad in "fur and red silk" and a "great, sparkling crown". The close focus on the bodily appearance of the Viking and his physicality is of course related to the historical construction of the Viking as a reaver, warrior, and barbarian, and its long-standing function as a 'barbarian outsider' motif (Service 1998; Stadius 2001).

At the same time, however, the general excessiveness of the Viking body here, and the attention devoted to it, also recalls the centrality of the masculine, brawny body to the action film. Emerging in the 80s Hollywood action cinema, the built, immensely muscular, body of the male hero emerged, in the words of Yvonne Tasker, as "the evolution of a previously unseen cinematic articulation of masculinity", which simultaneously "echoed unsettling images from the past, through their implicit invocation of a fascist invocation of the idealisation of the white male body" (Tasker 1993, 1).

Tasker understands action cinema as hinging on the glorification of hardbody masculinity through a narrative where that body becomes "the place of last resort [...] the sole space that is safe", even as this space is "constantly under attack" (ibid., 65). According to her, the action narrative serves precisely to make a spectacle of this form of masculine embodiment, and does so through a narrative framing that allows this body to be shown off in dangerous and harsh situations and environments where it is brawn, and not brains, that exists as the only possible form of salvation. In so doing, the action film constructs a particular geography, which Tasker calls a "*home and hell*" geography (ibid., 98 [emphasis in original]). The supposed hell of the harsh wilderness is where the action hero is at home and thrives, and the home, a civilized place of safety and comfort, is hellish to him. This home and hell geography draws on a distinct demarcation between civilization and wilderness, center and margin, an opposition that serves to make a spectacle of the muscular action-hero body, viable only in the 'hellish' wilderness. In the fantasy text, the home and hell geography largely maps onto the established North–civilization dichotomy.

"Thought this was a civilized place": The Fantasy World and Power

In *The Red Queen's War*, we are introduced to Snorri in the heart of imperial power, in chains and enslaved, as an effect of a violent economic transaction, with little choice but to comply with the wishes of the empire's royal family. As soon as Jalan gets him into the gladiatorial pits, however, a place marked instead by violence, and unleashes him in the fighting ring where it is physical power that determines the day, Snorri is able to escape. Proving himself too effective against his human opponents, Snorri is set to fight a bear. When the bear is brought in, he asks to fight a bigger one: "You call that a bear? [...] I am Snorri, Son of the Axe. I have fought trolls! You have a bigger bear. I saw it back in the cells. Send that one" (Lawrence 2015a, 57). A polar bear is brought out and Snorri escapes by tricking the bear into letting him clamber on top of it:

> Roaring outrage, the bear snapped erect, reaching for the annoyance, powering up to its full height as if Snorri was a child and it the father carrying him aback. [...] Snorri ver Snagason surged through the highborn crowd, trampling grown men underfoot. [...] He was out into the street before half the crowd even knew what had happened. (Lawrence 2015a, 59)

Immediately, the structures of power are overturned, Snorri "trampling" the highborn "underfoot", instead of being chained by them, their blood and money unable to withstand the power inherent in his Viking body. Importantly, it is with the help of a bear "of some arctic breed" (Lawrence 2015a, 58) that Snorri manages to escape the confines of the empire and reverse its power dynamic. The fighting pit and the presence of the bear – described as having a familial relationship to Snorri, no less – invokes precisely the same home and hell geography as described by Tasker; it is because of the small slice of Northern wilderness represented here that Snorri suddenly has the upper hand and can escape the empire's clutches. In the turmoil of Snorri's escape, however, Jalan is captured by his enemies. Snorri eventually saves him, and, through a series of convoluted events, they are forced to embark on a quest to the North to save the world, which furthers the reversal of power between them in Snorri's favor.

Both the action cinema and the fantasy world build a spatial–symbolic landscape, which hinges, importantly, upon the contrast between institutionalized forms of power and power as embodied in the strong, muscular, masculine body. In Hollywood action cinema, this home and hell geography, and its relation to the action-hero body, is generally constructed in terms of American geopolitics and questions of belonging, nationhood, and identity. Here, the US has historically been constructed as the home to be protected and some far off jungle, often symbolic of Vietnam and the Vietnam war (Tasker 1993, 8–9), as the hell in which the action hero can simultaneously be displayed and constructed as protecting 'home'. Of course, the geopolitical relation between the North and the 'home' of civilization in these texts maps out differently, since, as previously outlined, the North is differently related in the Anglophone imagination.

In *Half the World* (*The Shattered Sea* #2), its Viking protagonists have travelled to a far-off empire. Unlike in *The Red Queen's War*, they are not there against their will, but are still made highly uncomfortable by the experience. As they step off the docks, they are met by a scene of wild scuffling amongst a crowd trying to get on a ship. "Thought this was a civilized place?" one of them mutters. Another sardonically replies that 'civilized' "mostly means folk prefer to stab each other in the back than the front". "'Less chance of getting blood on your fine robe that way' said Thorn, watching a man hurry down a wharf on tiptoe holding his silken skirts above his ankles" (Abercrombie 2015b, 235).

Where the North perhaps initially appears as the less civilized place, it comes across as more honorable and honest than the corrupt civilization, where people are just as violent as in the North, only hiding it beneath a polished exterior. In this sense, the relation between the North and civilization in the fantasy texts maps on to the same imaginary geography as in the action film. Here, the wild becomes an uncomplicated place where the strong, masculine body prevails, as opposed to the treacheries of civilization, which is always out to get or exploit you (Tasker 1993, 113).

For one of the Viking warriors, being in the imperial palace "opened up whole new gulfs of crippling inadequacy" (Abercrombie 2015b, 286). While not as restrictive as Snorri and Jalan find the Red March, this palace is also imbued with a sense of imprisonment. Stepping into a beautiful garden filled with costly and lovely birds, another Viking wonders "why they didn't fly away", only to realize that "they were all tethered to their perches with silver chains fine as spiders' threads" (ibid., 288). The character in question, describing herself as a "horror", wonders how she was even let into the pretty garden and thinks that the "guards looked as if they had the same question" (ibid., 289). Here, luxury and captivity are intimately connected, which further becomes linked to feelings of inadequacy and inferiority on the part of the Vikings.

However, the Vikings soon get their chance to prove their worth. They discover a plot to kill the new Empress, a young girl recently having succeeded her departed mother. The plot is concocted by her uncle who wants to usurp the throne, and they come across him as he is about to execute the deed:

> "Stay back!" someone shrieked. An older man in a gilded breastplate with a
> sheen of sweat across his face. He had the Empress Vialine about the neck, a
> jewelled sword to her throat, but it was too long for the task. "I am Duke
> Mikedas!" he bellowed, as if the name was a shield.
>
> But a name's just a name. Brand's lips curled back and he took a step forwards,
> the growling in his throat hot as dragon's fire [...] His arms closed tight about
> the duke like a lock snapping shut. [...] He hoisted Duke Mikedas into the air
> as if he was made of straw. (Abercrombie 2015, 308–309)

Here, the primacy of the Viking body becomes evident when Brand can rely
on nothing but his great strength and berserker nature ("growling in his
throat hot like dragon's fire"), while the duke ("shriek[ing]", notably, rather
than "growling") attempts instead to shield himself behind his royal name,
since his overly decorated breastplate and sword are not up to "the task". As
we can see, the excessive masculine embodiment of the Viking is always
relational, established in relation to place as well as other men in a reiteration
of a civilization–wilderness dichotomy. Furthermore, it is ultimately the
Viking body that prevails, saving itself from both possible subordination and
captivity.

This centrality of the Viking body, as well as the Viking character itself,
emerges repeatedly in direct contrast to characters and places representing
institutional forms of power. However, the characters, places, and structures
representative of these institutional forms of power are also invested, quite
literally, with symbols of wealth and riches. The contrast between institutional and embodied power represented by the medieval West and/or
civilization and the Viking has an evident economic dimension. For Duke
Mikedas,[26] his richly decorated armor and sword connotate not only status
and power, but also excessive, needless wealth – all ultimately useless against
the naturalized strength of the Viking. The duke is easily killed by Brand, and
Empress Vialine instated as the region's rightful ruler.

Similarly, when we are introduced to Snorri in *The Red Queen's War*, he
finds himself in the heart of the imperial power of the Red March, not
foremost because of the empire's superior power or reach, but mainly
because of an economic transaction – of having been sold into slavery after
having been defeated by another Viking warrior, described as evil and
corrupt. Likewise, it is Jalan's economic dependency and debts that drive him

---

[26] The name holds a curious likeness to King Midas of Greek mythology, who was cursed by his wish
to turn things to gold with his bare hands.

to take note of Snorri, as well as the reason why he comes across as such a failed man, and his loser masculinity is further accentuated precisely by Snorri's spectacular Viking masculinity. The masculine Viking embodiment at once emerges in contrast to the depraved civilization, even as it also makes civilization meaningful in such a way through its naturalized, embodied power.

Jalan is eventually and very unwillingly dragged to the North. If the cold, harsh North is the hell in which Snorri is at home, it is only hellish for Jalan, whose masculinity and princely power is not viable outside the confines of the Red March. Jalan struggles greatly in the wild and the cold, and is ultimately dependent upon Snorri for everything, including staying alive. Snorri frequently has to shield Jalan from danger, or carry him around after he's been wounded, to Jalan's highly ambivalent consternation: "Now, I am not a man who finds pleasure in other men, but in that moment Snorri's over-muscled and sweaty embrace was a thousand times more welcome than any I might get from Cherri or Lisa. He hefted me over one shoulder and started walking" (Lawrence 2015a, 205). And: "I appeared to have been slung over someone's back. 'Put me down!' 'If you want'. Snorri's voice, very close to my ear. 'But it's probably better I wait until we're at the top. It's a long drop from here and you might damage something important' [...] I tightened my arms around Snorri's neck [...]" (Lawrence 2016, 431).

In fact, the journey to the North effectively and actively *disempowers* Jalan: in addition to being potentially lethal, the North strips him not only of his princely but also his masculine privilege. Despite Jalan's insistence that he finds no "pleasure in other men", there is a decidedly homoerotic dimension to his relationship with Snorri, centered around, notably, Snorri's Viking physique. It is because of his strength and might Snorri thrives in the wilderness so inimical to Jalan, which effectively constructs Jalan as the damsel to Snorri's hero. It is also Snorri's Viking strength that causes Jalan to jealously obsess over Snorri's well-muscled body, and in his keen attempts to keep interested women away from Snorri often seems to confuse whether he wishes to keep the women for himself, or Snorri.

Furthermore, when stopping in a village along the way, Jalan goes out drunk alone at night and is suddenly made aware of another person noticing him: "[...] I could make out a cloaked figure in the gloom. I stood, blinking, hoping to God that this wasn't some horny but myopic clansman who was going to attempt to carry me off to a distant village even more depressing than Harrowheim" (Lawrence 2015b, 57). In another scene, he is cornered by a man and dragged into a room at an inn. He is terrified that he will be sexually assaulted – until he realizes that the man in question is a cross-dressing woman, and instead becomes an enthusiastic and willing participant (Lawrence 2015a, 275–276).

These differences between Jalan and Snorri's respective masculinities and how they, respectively, connect to place are central to Lawrence's text (as well as the rest of the material, which I return to in chapter three). Jalan is repeatedly described as vain, lazy, physically inept, and lacking in honor, while Snorri's fearsome warrior skills, communicated through his physically strong body, and his manly and honorable quest for revenge, is emphasized. Jalan is a prince, whatever power he commands given to him by hereditary and imperial decree; Snorri a commoner, his place in the world shaped by his will and his own two hands. For both of them, the empire, represented by the Red March's throne room and its lack of escape routes, comes across as stifling. While Snorri stands chained as the result of betrayal and the immense and economic power of the Red March, Jalan has forged his chains by himself, through his decadence; his poor decision-making, lewd conduct, and gambling have made him despised by his own family and imperiled by those he owes money to. Even so, and despite his momentary fantasy of wanting "to be a Viking too, swinging my axe on a longboat" (Lawrence 2015a, 26), the wild North is ultimately hostile to Jalan.

The juxtaposition of Jalan and Snorri – the barbarian versus the effete, aristocratic Southerner – mirrors the spatial and symbolic relationality of the fantasy North and civilization or the medieval West, turning on a number of dichotomies: not only margin and center, savage and civilized, but also power as embodied (in the Viking body) versus systemic (represented here by the aristocracy, empire, and the economy).

Hanna-Riikka Roine writes: "I see speculative worldbuilding as a way of turning abstract and general thought experiments (or ideas) into a particular and therefore communicable form. [...] In this sense, the study of worldbuilding is not only about how the works of fiction invite us to engage with them, but also about how they seek engagement with the world" (Roine 2016, 18–19). Through the relationality of the Viking/North and the civilization/the medieval West and its inhabitants, the fantasy world clearly contrasts and works through different conceptualizations of power – located in the geopolitics of the fantasy world, as well as its characters. Here, the contrast between power as embodied in the masculine Viking (originating, importantly, in the cold, harshness of the wild North), and power as institutional, represented by civilization, empire, and monarchy emerge as the central divide.

However, this dichotomy is also a triangulation; the representation of power extending not only to relations between men or between different parts of the fantasy world, but also to questions of female power and women as powerful agents in systems of power that both historically and generally in fantasy literature have been understood as patriarchal. Interestingly, female power is both bound up with the dichotomy of power as embodied versus institutional, but also exists outside it.

In *The Red Queen's War*, institutional power and female power are aligned, as any real power within the Red March lies with women: with Jalan's grandmother, who won the throne through military conquest in her youth, and her successor, Serah, as violent and willful as she is beautiful. Here, Jalan's ineptitude is enforced not only in relation to Snorri, but also in comparison to more powerful women.

In *The Shattered Sea*, however, the young empress might be a regent of a mighty empire, but she needs protection from the Vikings against the covert, wrongful, and greedy machinations of that same empire. Here, it is the sexist attitude[27] of the vainglorious Duke Mikedas that becomes construed as emblematic of the depravity of civilization, and the instating of Vialine as its possible rehabilitation into something less problematic. I will discuss the fantasy heroine and how she figures in relation to conceptualizations of power in the material more closely in the next chapter. Suffice to say, this far, gender cuts through the literalization and materialization of power in the fantasy world in complex ways.

---

[27] When attempting to defend his actions, the duke argues that he tries to kill his niece because she is a young girl he cannot control: "We all like a girl with spirit, don't we? [...] But there is a limit. Really there is" (Abercrombie 2015b, 298).

Chapter 3: No Future for Vikings – Temporality and Homosociality

Just as the world is central to fantasy, so is the journey across it. As Diana Wynne Jones notes, the ubiquitous fantasy map serves both as an introduction to the world and as a clue to the plot; only areas relevant to and visited during the story are included (Jones 2006, xi). The dominant form of the epic fantasy is the hero's journey (Campbell 1949/2004), with the hero setting out across the world with the aim of restoring it.

Gritty fantasy has been understood as a deconstruction of not only earlier forms of epic fantasy but also the hero's journey itself, which it deliberately sets out to frustrate or subvert (see, for example, Sedlmayr 2014; Petzold 2017; Carroll 2018). From this perspective, the hero's journey in gritty fantasy is ultimately futile, leading to no moral development, effecting little or no change for the world, with the long and often bloody trek across the fantasy land only furthering its pointlessness.

On Joe Abercrombie's *The First Law*, Gerold Sedlmayr writes:

> Although the trilogy is constructed according to a circular pattern (Logen's fall in the first and last chapter), this is not the traditional regenerative cycle of life – death – life. There is no proper development. […] While the characters have altered physically, it is highly questionable whether their alteration also bears an inner – a 'moral' – quality. (Sedlmayr 2014, 176)

This holds true not only for *The First Law*, but the majority of texts in my material. Near the end of *The Red Queen's War*, after a transformative journey into the North, Jalan returns to his decadent ways, the closing scene in the final installment of the series an almost exact mirror of the beginning in the first. In *The Shattered Sea*, its heroes manage to salvage the world from tyrannical rule only to install it themselves instead, while the heroes of *A Land Fit for Heroes* at the end are either dead or worse off than when they began. *The Iskryne Saga* is an exception, aiming at subverting fantasy tropes other than its good–evil morality as embodied in the righteous hero; I will return to this in the next chapter.

In reading the action film, Yvonne Tasker argues against "an inordinate emphasis on the operations of narrative [...] the significance often given to the moment of narrative resolution as a way to decode the politics of a given text" (Tasker 1993, 6). For her, "the 'action' of action cinema refers to the enactment of spectacle *as* narrative [...]" (ibid. [emphasis in original]). Part of this spectacle is, of course, the action-hero body itself, but also the setting that allows for the display of that same body (see chapter two). In this chapter, I consider what happens when characters cross into or out of the North, how this relates to the establishment of close homosocial relationships across these boundaries, and what they come to entail in the texts.

Between Vikings and Other Men

In the previous chapter, I discussed the homoerotic dimensions of Prince Jalan and the Viking Snorri's relationship in *The Red Queen's War*. This tendency is perhaps best exemplified by a scene in which Jalan has been wounded and has to be carried around in "Snorri's over-muscled and sweaty embrace" and enjoys it immensely, even while he firmly contends that he is "not a man who finds pleasure in other men" (Lawrence 2015a, 205). Snorri and Jalan's relationship in many ways perfectly encapsulates the basic relationality of the North as contrasted to the medieval West, the wild periphery next to the corrupt civilization. Where Snorri relies predominantly on his own strength and skill in battle, Jalan's masculine privilege instead hinges upon his position as prince, which utterly fails in the wilderness of the North. Instead, his journey into the North and his close association with Snorri actively disempowers him, and even feminizes him to some extent.

In *Between Men: English Literature and Male Homosocial Desire* (1985), Eve Kosofsky Sedgwick introduces the idea of queer potentiality within close relations between men. She challenges the clear-cut demarcation between platonic and sexual relationships between men, and the construction of the heterosexual man as completely divorced from that of the homosexual. Instead, she understands male homosociality as a spectrum including all close relationships between men. Central to her readings is the figure of the erotic triangle, by which representations of close relations between men are structured and (supposedly) absolved of the threat of homosexuality through the inclusion of rivalry over a woman.

Examining literature from Shakespeare to the 19th century, Sedgwick writes of the historical period she studies: "the emerging pattern of male friendship, mentorship, entitlement, rivalry, and hetero- and homosexuality was in an intimate and shifting relationship to class; and [...] no element of that pattern can be understood outside of its relation to women and the gender system as a whole" (Sedgwick 1985, 1). The main focus of Sedgwick's analysis is the 19th and early 20th centuries, a period that saw the consolidation of the categories of homo- and heterosexual, and was structured by intense homophobia and misogyny.

In "Becoming Bromosexual: Straight Men, Gay Men, and Male Bonding on U.S. TV" (2014), Ron Becker argues that changes in societal acceptance of same-sex relationships have altered how male homosociality is structured in relation to homosexuality and homophobia in cultural representations. Looking at contemporary US television, Becker finds that as homosexuality becomes more visible, straight men can engage in close, intimate friendships – so called bromances – without the fear of either being considered gay, or of the close male friend having romantic or sexual, rather than platonic, motivations:

> As the cultural visibility of gay men and social acceptance of homosexuality become a new normal [...] it becomes easier to operate under the assumption, however naïve, that all gay men are out and that any man who is not out is straight. Within this logic, straight masculinity and straight men become less threatened by homosexuality and by accusations of being gay [...] [C]onstructions of hegemonic masculinity may remain thoroughly linked to heterosexuality and even more so to rigid notions of gender difference, but the bromance discourse suggests that the perceived tension between the imperatives to bond with other men and to be heterosexual may be abating. (Becker 2014, 250)

How the relationship between male homosociality, homosexuality, and "the gender system as a whole" (Sedgwick 1985, 1) is structured has in other words been subject to change – as we can see in how Jalan can utilize and take obvious pleasure in Snorri's "over-muscled and sweaty embrace", even preferring it to his female lovers', by contending that he is straight, and not gay (Lawrence 2015a, 205).

However, an important point for Sedgwick is how male homosociality is always connected to class, gender, and power. For her, homosocial relationships between men are fraught not only with the possibility of subsumed eroticism, but also hierarchization and power imbalances: "The homosociality of this world seems embodied fully in its heterosexuality; *and its shape is not that of brotherhood, but of extreme, compulsory, and intensely volatile mastery and subordination.*" (Sedgwick 1985, 66 [my emphasis]) She continues: "[…] for a man to undergo even a humiliating change in the course of a relationship with a man still feels like *preserving or participating in a sum of male power*, while for a man to undergo any change in the course of a relationship with a woman feels like a radical degeneration of substance" (ibid., 45 [my emphasis]). Sedgwick's point is that homosocial relationships between men are structured by power, not only in relation to women but also specifically *between* men; male homosociality is constituted by power inequalities among men, and these power inequalities, of the superiority of some men in relation to others, do not threaten the "sum of male power", but rather work to uphold it.

According to Tasker, the spectacular display of the action-hero body and his excessive physicality is directly connected to the question of class. The primacy of the strong, masculine body connotates the action hero with working-class masculinity, and, furthermore, the recurring action narrative of the triumph of this form of masculinity, individualized in the image of the muscular body, relates to a classed experience of being reduced to the body – an experience that, within the action cinema, becomes glorified. The action hero "express[es] the powerlessness of the 'ordinary soldier' […] whilst at the same time [offering up], in the figure of the muscular hero, an extraordinary soldier" (Tasker 1993, 100).

Valerie Walkerdine has written similarly on the action cinema and its glorification of violence that it "relates not only to masculinity, but also to lived oppression, to the experience of powerlessness and the fear of it" (Walkerdine 1999, 192). The action hero, and the action film, is at the same time very strongly symbolic of masculinity *and* a vehicle for complex concerns of power and oppression, worked through the image of the muscular, masculine body always oscillating between being empowered *via* the body and reduced *to* a body.

In the fantasy text, the North becomes, in direct contrast to the civilized West, the place where the action-hero body of the Viking is displayed and, as Tasker puts it, "the last certain territory of the action narrative […] the place of last resort" (Tasker 1993, 151). For Tasker, the primacy of the body is related to the marginalization of voice and rationality; it is solely through the (ab)use of his body that the action hero triumphs. In the fantasy text, the primacy of the Viking body emerges in direct opposition to the institutionalized, aristocratic, and economic power of the medieval West.

In Abercrombie's *The Blade Itself* (*The First Law* #1), discussed in the previous chapter, the arrival of two Northmen envoys, mighty and scarred, is enough to frighten the realm's most formally powerful men into dumb silence. They are ultimately helpless to protect themselves against the North-men's threats, despite being in the heart of the Union's authority, surrounded by wealth, power, and guards. In the same text, nobleman Jezal dan Luther is equal parts horrified and scornful of Logen Ninefinger's scarred and muti-lated barbarian body, until they embark upon a quest into the wilderness, where Logen steps in as Jezal's mentor, teaching him to survive outside the confines of the Union. In *The Red Queen's War*, this divide is instead played for humor: Jalan uselessly fumbling his way through the wilderness, insisting on being deferred to as a prince, even as it is clear that he holds no power outside of his grandmother's kingdom.

Myles Balfe, in his analysis of orientalism in fantasy literature, under-stands the medieval West as the moral center of the fantasy world and texts (Balfe 2004). The medieval West is, as previously discussed, the center of these gritty fantasy worlds and the texts, but seldom comes across as *moral*. A salient difference between the texts Balfe discusses and gritty fantasy is precisely the question of morality: while traditional fantasy has long hinged upon a good–evil dichotomy, which often turns, furthermore, upon raciali-zation and othering (see Loponen 2019), gritty fantasy instead takes place in a morally bankrupt world filled with corrupt people.

Even so, some sort of moral difference is obvious in the clear discrepancies between Jalan and Snorri – between the spoilt, vain, and ostentatious prince next to the long-suffering and honor-bound Snorri, whose only faults seem to be a propensity for extreme violence and being a bit dumb. The harsh North becomes not only a naturalized wilderness that serves to display and make vital the hardbody physicality of the Viking, in contrast to the 'hellish home' of civilization. It also serves to make certain forms of masculinities more legitimate than others; through the homosocial relationship between Snorri and Jalan, male power as located in the muscular, physical power of the Viking becomes righteous, necessary, and vital, compared to the useless and self-serving, situational power of the aristocratic Jalan, symbolic of the wider corruption, uselessness, and power-hunger of the civilized center.

On the Gothic, Sedgwick writes on the role of the aristocracy as a motif: "An important, recurrent, wishful gesture of this ideological construction was the femininization of the aristocracy as a whole, by which [...] the abstract image of the entire class, came to be seen as ethereal, decorative, and otiose in relation to the vigorous and productive values of the middle class" (Sedgwick 1985, 93). The Viking, naturally, connotates a rather different set of class values.

Alexandra Service reads the popular Viking primarily as a barbarian motif. She understands the barbarian motif is a larger cultural-historical motif of civilization, self, and otherness and how, in particular, hegemonic powers have used the barbarian other to define themselves. Like the North, oscillating between utopia and savagery, this motif is at once loaded with positive and negative meanings of the barbarian as both enemy and rejuvenator of civilization: "Barbarians are foreign, those seen as essentially different. They are the enemy, civilisation's opponents, but they can equally be more noble and virtuous than degenerate civilisation" (Service 1998, 120–121). In the same way that Kristin Loftsdottír understands the Northern wilderness as a utopian *and* savage landscape (Loftsdóttir 2015), the Viking, Service shows, shifts between the role of hero and villain in relation to civilization: it can either function as an enemy horde or an inspiring alternative.

In the homosocial relationship between the effete aristocratic Jalan and the hardbody barbarian Snorri, we can see a "wishful gesture of ideological construction" similar to Sedgwick's description that posits this fantasy aristocracy as corrupt and useless next to the working class-connotated, physical hardbody of the barbarian Viking. Sedgwick discusses the Gothic and its representation of male homosociality against the background of its historical context, more precisely the rise of the bourgeoise in the 19th century. The contemporary context is, of course, rather different. What then does this very similar "wishful gesture" of the strong barbary Viking placed next to the decadent ruling elite come to mean and what effects does this have in the contemporary fantasy text?

"Out Here in the Frozen Wilderness": Place, Body, and Agency

Much like *The Red Queen's War*, space, place, and homosocial relationships in Joe Abercrombie's *The First Law* hinge upon a spatial–symbolic divide between the barbarian North and the civilized medieval West. The particular medieval West of this text is the Union, which has been weakened by years of corruption and mismanagement by its ruler and aristocracy. Its king is old and ill, and his oldest son and heir, Ladisla, is another Jalan-figure: lazy, decadent, and cowardly, with little concern for the reality of leading a kingdom but enamored with the power and status it grants him.

The Union is being dragged into two wars: one with the North, which wants to take back lands previously annexed by the Union, and one with the empire of Gurkhul attempting to invade from the South. In the North, a man called Bethod is attempting to unify its many scattered clans under his own banner. Proclaiming himself King of the Northmen, he seeks to modernize the region and wants to recover what the Union once conquered. The story is told from the point of view of a range of characters, but most important to my discussion here is a band of grizzled but fearsome Northman warriors opposed to Bethod, and a Union man they come into contact with in *Before They Are Hanged* (*The First Law* #2): Corporal Collem West, a long-suffering soldier in the Union army sent North to resist Bethod's army.

Among the storied warriors, hardened killers, powerful wizards, lofty kings, and conspiratorial torturers of Abercrombie's trilogy, West stands out as the sole 'everyman' character. As one of the text's few more or less well-intentioned characters, he is the only one not ultimately revealed as morally bankrupt or tragically corrupted during the course of the story. He is, importantly, a commoner who has painstakingly made his way into a position as a highly ranked officer in the Union army, fighting against prejudice and his lack of aristocratic blood all the way. His main prerogative is to do the best he can by the men he leads and the self-destructive sister he is responsible for, and to avoid turning into his father, a violent and abusive man.

This biography, taken together with his name, "West", makes him easy to read as a metaphor for the transformative journey of the medieval West into the North. He is also, notably, born in Angland, the Northern territory previously annexed by the Union. Despite undoubtedly loyal to the Union, West's status in the text as an everyman character is reinforced by the fact that he is of the liminal area of Angland, a rural Union outpost annexed to secure lumber and steel, rather than of the Union proper, with all its civilized, aristocratic decadence and corruption.

West finds himself lost in the snowy North after a disastrous battle against the superior Northmen with Prince Ladisla – the leader of the army and foremost cause of said disaster – in tow. Eventually, West and Ladisla happen upon a band of outlawed Northmen warriors, who allow West and, at West's insistence, Ladisla to accompany them through the hostile wintry woods. For West, the trek through the cold North is rough and he wonders at the strength of the Northmen: "The Northmen were machines, every one of them. Men carved from wood who never got tired, who felt no pain" (Abercrombie 2007, 308). West does not quite have the strength to keep up, and is also in charge of Ladisla, honor-bound to make sure the prince returns home unscathed. The Northmen would prefer to leave him behind since they deem him useless as he, in West's words, "stumbl[es] daintily through the mud with a petulant frown on his face" (ibid., 313).

Where the dichotomy of masculine power as embodied versus institutionalized was played out in the close homosocial relationship between Snorri and Jalan in *The Red Queen's War*, here West instead oscillates between these two poles, initially balanced in the middle: retaining the discipline and hierarchy of his military training and his loyalty to the Union crown, while petitioning the Northmen for help and surreptitiously agreeing with their low estimation of Ladisla.

As the journey through the frozen woods continues, this balance shifts. Despite the many hardships, West's spirits seem to rise during the sojourn in the North: "The situation was dire, but against all reason, West's heart felt light. The fact was, out here, things were simple. There were no daily battles to be fought, prejudices to be overcome, no need to think more than an hour ahead. He felt *free* for the first time in months" (ibid., 316 [my emphasis]).

In his discussion of heroism in *The First Law*, Jochen Petzold also notes the significance of the juxtaposition of the North and the Union:

> [...] both the Union and the North revere a heroism that is built on notions of manliness, courage, physical strength and military prowess, although closer inspection reveals significant differences between the two societies. [...] While the social structure of the North rewards heroism by upward social mobility, in the Union, the reverence of heroes and heroism is mainly for show and cannot break social stratification. (Petzold 2017, 141–142)

What West has become "free" from in the cold, freezing North, then, is precisely the stratified class society of the Union where a man as ostentatious as Ladisla, depicted as an unmanly, vain, and selfish idiot, is worth more than a decent, hardworking, self-made man like West. The Northmen are completely baffled by West's continued dedication to the prince, asserting that they would not "piss on him if he was burning", since in the North leaders are chosen "because of what they'd done, not whose son they were" (Abercrombie 2007, 277).

As Petzold writes, where in the Union social positions are cemented by blood and formal power structures, social hierarchization is more malleable in the North, where it is predicated instead upon physical strength, toughness, and prowess in battle. Consequently, while homosocial – or any – relationships in the Union are all shaped by barriers of class, in the North these relationships are based on, if not always friendship, at least mutual respect. To put this in Sedgwick's terms (1985, 66): in the North, the mastery and subordination of the Union's aristocratic structure is supposedly dissolved in favor of brotherhood. However, ultimately this brotherhood only substitutes the institutionalized hierarchization of aristocracy and class with that of embodied strength.

As they run into a band of enemy Northmen, West is called upon to fight with the Northmen. Ladisla is left behind, notably with Cathil, the only girl in the group. In order to flank the enemy, West and one of the Northmen have to pass through a stream. The Northman wades through it easily, but West has a harder time of it: "He would have screamed if the freezing water had not hammered the air out of his lungs. He floundered forward, half-stumbling, half-swimming, teeth gritted with panic, sloshed up onto the far bank [...] The Northman smirked at him. 'You look cold, boy'" (ibid., 358).

The fight, however, quickly warms him up. Going into a berserker rage, West kills several opponents, loses his sword, and ends up biting an enemy's nose off. This both amuses and impresses the Northmen: when the fighting is over the Northman who teased West for looking cold, nicknames him "Furious". Through his literal baptism in the icy water and the hot blood of the North, West has become a Northman, taken up among the warrior brotherhood as a Named Man, a Northern warrior given a name from his deeds in battle. On the way back he "wade[s] across the stream almost without noticing the cold" (ibid., 361); unlike the Union man floundering his way across before the battle, he can now, like any Northman, not only prove himself in battle, but also easily enforce the region's icy hostility.

Additionally, he has freed himself from the constraints of civilization. As they return to camp, they find Ladisla attempting to rape Cathil, and, in a rage, West throws him off a cliff. He is at once horrified and resigned: "The sunny [Union], where loyalty and deference were given without question, where commoners did what their betters told them, where the killing of other people were simply not the done thing, all this was very far away. Monster he may be, but, out here in the frozen wilderness [...], the rules were different" (ibid., 363). Freed from social stratification of the Union, he can finally act according to his own moral compass.

The killing of Ladisla mirrors an earlier scene in the trilogy, where West was overcome with the same righteous anger. At that time, it was aimed at the ineffectuality and banal cruelty of the Union's military bureaucracy which caused the men under West's command to be sent to the North improperly outfitted due to an economic deficit, the oversight explained away by obscure administrative jargon. Immobilized by the impermeability of government, he returns home only to discover that his sister, Ardee, has been having pre-martial relations with a nobleman. In his anger, he strikes her. His anger is not truly directed at her, but at the unfair power structure of the Union, represented by its careless military bureaucracy and its nonchalant aristocracy, taking advantage of both West's soldiers and his sister.

In the "sunny" Union, West is helpless to do anything but inadvertently prop up the classed and patriarchal stratification of civilization, going along with the military's impossible demands and disciplining Ardee for her illicit sexuality. In the barbarian North, however, he forcefully opposes those same structures, through the use of righteous, sovereign violence. When trying to affect change in the Union, West again and again comes up against its gargantuan and ineffectual machinery, portrayed as more or less a helpless cog, unable to do much but comply. In the North, however, one single decisive action is suddenly enough to dramatically alter both his own circumstances and those of Ladisla's intended victim – as well as the very heart of the Union's power.

The Viking or Northmen in these texts are powerful avatars of agency, and the wilderness of the North the place where this agency is best displayed and utilized. This agency, in turn, hinges upon masculine power as located in the physically strong body, given free rein in the harsh North. It is, curiously, both firmly embodied in the strong Viking body, and, to some extent, transitory: the Vikings, or Northmen, are, after all, self-made men, and so West, too, can remake himself in the North, modelling himself on their ethos. Even so, he remains apart, inexorably bound to the Union, and tragically has to return eventually. The wishful gesture of this homosocial construction is not foremost symbolic of changes in class relations, as in Sedgwick's discussion of the Gothic, but rather constructs a fantasy of autonomy and sovereignty: there *is* an outside to structural, institutional power, located in the physically powerful male body of the Viking, and accessed in the harsh wilderness of the North.

The Viking Beyond Civilization and Modernity

Unlike Tasker's action hero, the Viking is not a contemporary figure, but rather a figure directly connoted with ideas of the past (see Wilkins 2016). So far, I have foremost discussed the Viking and the North in terms of spatiality, but the question of temporality is also highly central in these texts. The construction of the fantasy world in terms of center and margin, civilization and wilderness, the civilized medieval West and the Viking barbarian, is not only a matter of place and space, but also of time and temporal linearity.

The term 'civilization' has here been called upon to represent a wide variety of institutionalized forms of power in these texts – ranging from empire, kingdom, the aristocracy, the military, bureaucracy, to the economy. These are of course very different forms of governance that in this discussion have been purposefully aligned under the heading of 'civilization', and are mainly synonymous with the medieval West, since I understand their importance in these texts foremost in relation to their antithesis: the embodied power and agency of the barbarian Viking.

West's personal transformation and triumph in the North ends when he returns to the Union. Back after the failed campaign, West is promoted to marshal. Despite this elevated position, he remains bereft of any real agency. When Gurkhul finally attempts its invasion of the Union in the final battle of the trilogy, they are repelled by the wizard Bayaz, who unleashes a powerful spell upon the enemy. The spell does not, however, distinguish between friend and foe, and along with the invasion force, scores of Union soldiers succumb to what seems to the reader like radiation poisoning. West is among the casualties, dying a gruesome and drawn-out death from friendly fire.

The character of Bayaz is key to understanding the questions of power, agency, masculinity, and temporality raised in *The First Law* (cf Sedlmayr 2014). Bayaz is the primary antagonist of the text, a megalomanic wizard[28] controlling large parts of the world, and by pulling the strings of its leaders through loans issued from his bank, Valint & Balk. Bayaz represents or even incarnates a budding capitalist system in the medievalist fantasy world, controlling the world through money and leveraged interest.[29] Notably, it is in the North Bayaz has most difficulty securing his foothold: he controls Bethod, the man trying to make himself king by uniting and modernizing the region through centralizing the North. However, both Bayaz's and Bethod's respective handles on the North fail at the close of *The Last Argument of Kings*

---

[28] An evident subversion of the benign wizard guide trope, its most evident example Tolkien's Gandalf.

[29] Recall also the role played by money in *The Red Queen's War*: it is, above all, his terrible finances and inability to handle money that forces Jalan onto the quest with Snorri (whose initial victimization, furthermore, consist of being sold into slavery, his life reduced to an economic transaction). During the course of their travels, it is often money that gets Jalan into trouble. These troubles do not cease until Jalan, in the final novel, returns home and brutally kills the moneylender to whom he owes money, using his skills earned through his travels with Snorri in the North to end the problem for good through violent means, not unlike West's handling of Ladisla.

(*The First Law* #3), when Logen Ninefingers first defeats Bethod's champion in a duel and then beats Bethod himself to death with his bare hands.

Following this brutal act of physical violence, Bayaz's control on the North slips until, later in the series, Bethod's son Calder eventually regains his father's lost position. Calder is described as a highly unusual Northman, concerned with his looks and expensive clothes bought from outside the region, and with little or no skills in battle. Instead, he schemes his way into power, making his brother – a mighty warrior with very little brains – king, while he controls the throne from the shadows. It is symptomatic that it is this cosmopolitan, political man who falls under Bayaz's control, and not his brawny, battle-hardened brethren. It is the double threat of modernity and commerce that allow Bayaz a foothold in the otherwise resistant North, and it is their dependence and reverence for brute force that is the source of that resistance. Bayaz can control large-scale flows of money, industries, armies, and political power, but he cannot stop one lone, strong man from beating another to death with his bare hands.

Richard Morgan's *A Land Fit for Heroes* trilogy reiterates the same barbarian/civilization juxtaposition and its relation to homosociality, but to some extent these divisions are somewhat less spatially fixed. Instead, it is temporality that is at the forefront. "Not this again", its protagonist, Ringil Eskiath, mutters at the opening of *The Steel Remains* (*A Land Fit for Heroes* #1) (Morgan 2008, 3) when his heroic skills are needed, immediately framing the text in terms of the narrative sterility characteristic of gritty fantasy. The text plays not only with heroism, but also with time and modernity. This is a bleak fantasy world where the Southern empire of Yhelteth entered into a tenuous alliance with the medieval West, Trelayne, during a war against dragons from across the sea, which was then narrowly won. Since the war, the alliance is mainly an economic one, lubricated by trade in slaves.

The North supposedly stands outside all this, but some ambitious Majaks – unable to take control through violent revolt, the more customary and honorable way – have allied themselves with Yhelteth, seeking to empower themselves by assassinating the tribes' current leaders. Like in *The First Law*, the North stands outside the conflicts of the great powers, even as its autonomy is eroded by betrayal from political men (and notably not warriors) from within. These conflicts are complicated by the threat of the dwenda, an otherworldly enemy that once ruled the continent and has returned beyond time to conquer it anew. The dwenda (a gritty reflection of Tolkien's elves) are a remnant from the past within the text (and a reference to the romanticism and nostalgia of post-Tolkienian fantasy), in juxtiposition to the economic-religious-societal conflicts that form the backdrop to the plot.

Of the three protagonists – one from each region – two are same-sex attracted, and are curiously suspended outside or in conflict with the medievalist temporality of the fantasy world. Ringil Eskiath has been disowned by his noble family and the Trelayan military because of his sexuality, and he finds himself unwillingly allied with the dwenda, seduced by one of them and removed into a parallel dimension outside of time. Here he encounters visions of alternate timelines, many of them where he is free to live without condemnation and in which his boyhood lover was never executed for sodomy. Archeth Indamaninarmal, on the other hand, is immortal and quite literally from another time, descended from a line of highly technologically advanced people from what might be a future version of our own world. Next to these two untimely figures is Northman Egar Dragonbane, firmly fixed in this medievalist 'past' as "a legend emerging from battlefield mist" (Morgan 2008, 292). Unlike his friends, he is incongruent only with its budding modernity.

For West, the journey into the North entailed freedom and sovereignty, while upon return to civilization he becomes a casualty, deemed a necessary sacrifice by his own side, killed, notably, by the untimely effects of radiation sickness. West does not die gloriously in hand-to-hand combat on a medievalist battlefield; rather his death brings to mind the horrors of a thoroughly modern battlefield. Unlike West, Egar moves in the opposite direction: away from the North where he has been leader of his tribe for the last few years, chafing at the responsibility all the while, to the South where he returns to an old lover and lives as her kept man for a while until he begins to long again for the North. Here he unites with Ringil and Archeth, setting off on a quest into the wild.

At the close of the series, the fellowship is attacked by a dragon, the last one left behind since the war decades ago. In the ensuing battle, Egar is killed, dying a glorious, heroic death to protect his companions and the quest. Like Abercrombie's Named Men, Egar earned 'Dragonbane' in his youth for his contributions to the war.[30] By dying in the battle with the final dragon, a literal remnant from the past, the circle is closed. Unlike West, Egar is not a casualty, but a *hero* – dying from his own gallant self-sacrifice, he avoids being caught up in the webs of power again, either as a leader or subject, while West dies

---

[30] Incidentally, Ringil failed to acquire the same title, despite performing the same deeds as Egar's comrade-in-arms, mistrusted by the rest of the men because of his homosexuality.

as a direct *consequence* of subjecting himself anew to the authority of the Union.

Where *The First Law* depicts an immersive medievalist world inexorably crumbling towards (Mendlesohn 2008, 113) modernity – that is, portrays a linearity of progress represented most directly by Bayaz and his economic hold, *A Land Fit for Heroes* instead brings into play the medieval and the modern as conflicting figures. Morgan's text determinedly establishes how bleak his medievalist world 'was': rife with violent homophobia, sexism, misuse of power, and general misery (cf Carroll 2018, 56). Ringil and Archeth, placed outside the time of the text, clearly establish a link to the present (Ringil with his visions of other possible timelines, Archeth as a descendant of the far future), their queerness and the precarity it brings within this medievalist world at once symptomatic of the horrors of this time as well as unreconcilable to it.

Next to them, Egar remains an uncomplicated figure of this past. While accosted by the ghosts of his parallel lives, Ringil even briefly entertains the idea of meeting another version of Egar: "He wondered vaguely if he'd meet some alternative Egar out under those aching, open skies. An Egar who's perhaps not quite so resolutely dedicated to pussy. There is a feeling in his chest now, dangerously close to longing. *What if…* He stamps down on it" (Morgan 2011, 169 [emphasis in original]). However, no glimpse of this alternative Egar emerges. Unlike the temporal fluidity seemingly inherent in the queer protagonists, the Viking remains firmly fixed in time. The relation between the North and the medieval West exists on a temporal axis as much as a spatial, the barbarian–civilization divide mirrored by a dichotomy of the past and the modern.

Examining the exoticized North in 19th century travel writing, Maria Lindgren Leavenworth understands the North to "represent a journey in time, back to a 'simpler' and more 'natural' life, untainted by the development associated with modernity […]" (Lindgren Leavenworth 2010, 7–8). Likewise, in the gritty fantasy text, the medieval West crumbles towards the future/present (evoked through such modern concepts as radiation sickness, contemporary conceptualizations of sexuality, and an emerging capitalist economy as a governing force), while the fantasy North remains more or less safely ensconced in the past. The journey North also becomes a journey into the past – or a way from the looming futurity – into something "'simpler' and more 'natural'", as Lindgren Leavenworth puts it. This pastness is furthermore located precisely in the masculine body locked in an adverse relationship to most forms of institutional power (Egar gladly leads battles but is miserable leading his tribe in peacetime) – the mighty Viking as simultaneously antithetical to civilization and the (threat of the) future.

Amy Kaufman has coined the term "muscular medievalism" as a way to interpret contemporary usage of the medieval, from *Game of Thrones* to the rhetoric of Donald Trump. "Behind such works of medievalism," Kaufman writes, "lurks the odor of nostalgic fantasy, a longing for the opposite side of the disempowered feminine equation: a muscular medievalism. Muscular medievalism imagines the past as a man's world in which masculinity was powerful, impenetrable, and uniquely privileged" (Kaufman 2016, 58). Kaufman discusses muscular medievalism particularly in relation to the predominance of sexual violence against women in the media she examines, and argues that the idea of the impenetrable, powerful masculinity needs to be understood in direct relation to these gratuitous displays of female vulnerability.

Much like Tasker's action hero, muscular medievalism emerges as the antidote or anthesis to (the fear of) vulnerability, an insistence on independence and autonomy, located in the powerful, self-reliant male body. This dichotomy exists on a temporal, as much as a gendered, axis, with this imaginary past supplying the arena for this performance of impenetrable masculinity supposedly denied or untenable in the present.

Adam Roberts further notes that gritty fantasy has much more to do with the present than with history (Roberts 2014, 39). As I've discussed, previous research has tended to emphasize gritty fantasy's orientation towards the past – both historical and to older forms of fantasy – but these are texts deeply concerned with the present moment, with questions of historical development, modernity, and changes in gender relations and sexuality at the fore, and with a particular focus on men and masculinities.

The medieval here exists as both counter *and* precursor to modernity, its empires and kings and absolute forms of power offering up the fantasy of muscular medievalism even as it gives way to the present that is in need of this "nostalgic fantasy", as Kaufman refers to it. Much like the North becomes a space of exotic wilderness supposedly untroubled by colonial power relations (Loftsdóttir 2015), the fantasy Viking is positioned as outside these troubling questions of modernity, autonomy, and power.

In both spatial and temporal terms, the Viking – and the North – here function as bulwarks against the movement towards the future/present. While these fantasy worlds are posited as inexorably moving from the medieval to the modern, the Viking and the North remain firmly anchored in the past, as spaces unstructured by institutional forms of power, where power instead derives directly from the physically strong, white, masculine body – constructed as a sovereign and more legitimate form of power.

"As a slave is chained to his mistress": Viking Agency and Female Empowerment

The Shattered Sea, Abercrombie's second series, can be read as the inverse of *The First Law*. Where *The First Law* tells the stories of characters at the mercy of Bayaz's world-spanning machinations, *The Shattered Sea* is about the making of the Bayaz-figure itself. The trilogy tells the story of Yarvi, a young boy and prince to the kingdom of Gettland, one of the many warring regions of this fantasy North. Born with a deformed hand and unable to wield a sword, Yarvi has been left out of the succession. Deemed less than a man, he has instead been set to train as a minister, a priest-adviser to the King and a role traditionally held by women. Ignored by his father, he is raised by the current minister, Mother Gundring, and his own mother, Laithlin, nick-named The Golden Queen because of the wealth she brings Gettland through her immense trading operations.

Yarvi becomes the eponymous half a king when his father and brothers are unexpectedly killed, leaving him the only heir. Not long after, he is betrayed by his uncle and sent off to die in battle. Yarvi manages to survive but is sold into slavery. He eventually frees himself, and journeys back home. He discovers that the death of his family members and his uncle's betrayal was part of a bigger plot, concocted by the High King, the mightiest regent in the North, and his minister, Grandmother Wexen, to subdue and unite the North and convert the region to the One God. Yarvi vows revenge, and the rest of the series is about the bloody conflicts Yarvi orchestrates to mobilize and unite one half of the North against the half controlled by the High King. Yarvi gains the nickname the Spider, because he is "lean and subtle and poisonous", spinning webs "for men and there was no telling who would be trapped in them" (Abercrombie 2015c, 62).[31]

During his struggle to return home in *Half a King* (*The Shattered Sea* #1), Yarvi encounters his other uncle, long presumed dead, and they return together. The uncle, Uthil, is installed as King and Yarvi becomes his advisor. Uthil is almost a caricature of stoic Viking manhood, repeatedly described as hard and unyielding as iron:

—

[31] Recall the silver chains, "fine as spider's threads" (Abercrombie 2015b, 288), that held the birds captive in the beautiful garden, discussed in chapter two, as symbolic of the threat of captivity and restriction represented by civilization.

> King Uthil stood tall and before them [...] cradling gently as a sick child his
> sword of plain grey steel. He needed no ornaments but the scars of countless
> battles on his face. Needed no jewels but the wild brightness in his eye. Here
> was a man who knew neither fear nor mercy. Here was a king that any warrior
> would be proud to follow [...]. (Abercrombie 2015c, 58)

His catchphrase, furthermore – seemingly applicable in any given situation –
is "Steel is the answer". However, Uthil may be "a king that any warrior would
be proud to follow", but it is Yarvi, supported by Queen Laithlin, who is the
true power behind the throne. Yarvi is not interested in the stability that
Uthil's coronation ostensibly brings. Instead, he secretly plots to unite the
North against the High King to get his vengeance.

In *Half a War* (*The Shattered Sea* #3), the princess Skara falls victim to
Yarvi's schemes when her kingdom is invaded by the enemy and her family
killed, leaving her a powerless heir in exile. She flees to Gettland, and unites
with King Uthil and another Viking king, Grom-gil-Gorm, against the High
King. Yarvi eventually wins the war, consolidating all the power in the North
under the pretext of resisting such a consolidation under the High King. He
tries to force Skara to marry his younger brother to join their two kingdoms
together, but Skara, who has realized what he's done, refuses, and instead
blackmails and manipulates him into confessing his crimes to her:

> She knelt before him, the chain of pommels rattling against her chest, and
> took his tear-stained face into her hands. Now she had to show her
> compassion. Her generosity. Her mercy. 'Listen to me [...] I know the weight
> of power and I do not judge you. But we must be together in this.'
>
> 'As a slave is chained to his mistress?' he muttered. [...] 'So we will dance into
> your bright future hand in hand, and keep the balance of the Shattered Sea
> between us. [...] It is hardly as if I have a choice, is it?' (Abercrombie 2015c,
> 477–478)

Unlike the other regents of the North – unbending Uthil, the berserker
warrior Grom-gil-Gorm, or the High King with his mighty army – Yarvi and
Skara are, by virtue of disability and gender, excluded from the warrior
homosociality that rules the North. Where Yarvi plots and schemes to get his
way, Skara likewise relies on her political acumen – and her marriageability
and 'feminine wiles'. The band of sword pommels "rattling against her chest"
in the quote above belongs to Grom-gil-Gorm, collected from all those he's
killed in battle. To gain him as an ally, she promises her hand in marriage
even as she is in love with one of his most trusted warriors, Raith. When Raith

is ordered to poison Skara, he instead serves his King the wine, killing him and leaving Skara to inherit the King's men and the symbols of his power, giving her the authority to (covertly) oppose Yarvi.

If *The First Law*, characteristic of early gritty fantasy, is about the cost of traditional forms of masculinity and its destructiveness for both men themselves and those that fall victim to it, *The Shattered Sea* instead specifically focuses on male homosociality as toxic – above all to those it excludes – and what these bonds cost to uphold.

Next to Yarvi and Skara we also have Thorn Bathu, a young woman training to be a warrior, derided by her peers as well as their trainer because of her gender. When she is goaded into a fight, she accidentally kills a fellow recruit and is set to be executed. Thorn's story of going her own way is a classic narrative of the fantasy heroine (Tolmie 2006; see chapter four for further discussion), but significant here is her love interest, Brand, who has to forsake the warrior brotherhood and the bonds of male homosociality to gain her love. Not only does he betray his friends by eventually telling the truth about what happened to Thorn, but he also speaks out against the use of excessive violence in battle, questioning the basis of what it means to be a man in this brutal society. Eventually he marries Thorn, settling into a rather domestic existence as the husband of his warrior wife.

Similarly, Raith forsakes the bonds of male homosociality for Skara – symbolized most clearly when he kills his King for her sake. He realizes that for all the honor Grom-gil-Gorm has supposedly offered him, he has really only been made into "a killer" (Abercrombie 2015c, 447). Thus, Raith murders him to save Skara's life, opting for poison, a weapon as underhanded as Yarvi and Skara's machinations, rather than the proper manly, homosocial way of the sword. Despite this, Skara eventually rejects Raith, since she needs a better marriage match than a lowly fighter. At this time, she is pregnant with his child, a fact of which he is unaware, and she eventually opts for an abortion to better rule her kingdom.

Reading *The First Law*, Sedlmayr understands it as a critique of capitalist body politics. Here he considers the representation of Bayaz as physically unimpressive and faintly ridiculous, and the fact that his immense power is not derived from the body – whether from strength or royal blood – as central. Furthermore, he reads the text, through Bayaz, as representative of a shift in how power is conceptualized in epic fantasy:

> What Bayaz stands for, then, is power, a power that is both invisible – you rarely become aware of the strings around your wrists – and decidedly

material. His actions illustrate, to borrow a phrase from Judith Butler, "the productive and, indeed, materializing effects of regulatory power" (910). In other words, the idea of power that the wizard Bayaz incorporates is one that strictly depends on an economics of power that is both beyond traditional moral distinctions and beyond the comprehension of the individual *actant*. (Sedlmayr 2014, 172, [emphasis in original])

Following Sedlmayr, I would say that in the medievalist worldbuilding of *The First Law*, Bayaz evokes a Foucauldian distinction between absolute and disciplinary power (see introduction for further discussion). The slow creep towards the future in these texts represents not only a movement towards modernity, or a temporal location, but also contrasts the absolute power of kings, associated by Michel Foucault with the medieval, to the disciplinary or regulatory mode of power as characteristic of the modern or postmodern. This is indeed vague and inexact, because of course these texts do not offer a sustained criticism of power in modernity, but instead contrast absolute and disciplinary modes of governing as a feature of worldbuilding. Through their temporal linearity – of the medievalist fantasy world crumbling towards the present and emphasizing this temporal link or flow – these texts evoke the Foucauldian distinction between the medieval and the modern as a way to make visible and evident shifting mechanisms of governing as a factor of worldbuilding (Bark Persson 2022).

According to Kaufman, muscular medievalism works through countering the fear of feminine vulnerability in modernity with a fantasy of the past in which masculinity was supposedly sovereign and impenetrable. What we can see here on the other hand is that modernity – the "bright future" that Skara will lead them into – is to some extent coded as feminine, but hardly connotated with powerlessness. Skara holds both Yarvi's strings and the people's, forcing them to "dance" for her, while Laithlin controls the region's flow of money; Bayaz split into two women.

In *The Red Queen's War*, Jalan's position is circumscribed by his powerful grandmother and her chosen heir, his much more accomplished cousin Serah. *The First Law* and *A Land Fit for Heroes* do indeed emphasize the victimization of women in the Middle Ages in accordance with what Kaufman describes, but no matter how powerful the (male) heroes, they all eventually come to the realization that they have been (mis)used by powers beyond their understanding, caught up in the same kind of webs that Yarvi and Skara spin.

Sedlmayr understands this as a critique of late-stage capitalism, while Roberts traces the barbaric medievalism of gritty fantasy to an experience of the present moment as "cynical, disillusioned [and] ultraviolent" (Roberts 2014, 39). Following the Viking and its position in relation to civilization, modernity, and gender in these texts, I argue that they revolve around a certain unease in regard to the *ephemerality of power*. The looming futurity becomes threatening foremost because it is associated with forms of power that supposedly render the embodied, sovereign, masculine power as located in the male body useless and obsolete.

In an appendix to *Half a King*, Abercrombie writes that the Viking Age setting of the series allowed him to include a lot of strong female characters (Abercrombie 2015a, 399). *The Shattered Sea* trilogy certainly offers up a wide variety of empowered female characters, as well as a sustained critique of the destructiveness of traditional forms of masculinity through characters like Brand and Raith. At the same time, these portrayals of female strength and male adaptability are also accompanied by certain anxieties regarding what this shift in power could possibly entail.

Yarvi and Skara's tactics alienate all their closest and more morally upstanding allies – Brand dies in a battle orchestrated by Yarvi, Skara forsakes Raith, and at the end of *Half a War*, Raith and Thorn both leave Gettland behind. They are the series' two most warlike characters, and them leaving simultaneously hammers home the horror of Yarvi and Skara's "[tyrant]" (Abercrombie 2015c, 459) reign, *and* maps onto the traditional action narrative. Tasker argues that the action film is episodic and open-ended, since to close the action narrative definitely down would be to derive the action hero of power – a defeat. Instead of settling down, Raith and Thorn are left to continue their adventures, conquered neither by a superior foe nor domesticity – nor, importantly, ultimately snared by Yarvi's and Skara's respective games of power.

Furthermore, while the text seems to champion a very modern view of female empowerment, the looming futurity still inspires disquiet in the text. *The Shattered Sea* takes place in a medievalist future, rather than past, after a cataclysmic event has devasted the world and apparently 'reset' it. Yarvi, Skara and their allies only win the final battle because they have managed to secure what they refer to as "elven" weapons – which to the reader is very clearly modern machine guns. With that amount of firepower, their victory is guaranteed. Even so, Skara is horrified by the ensuing slaughter:

> Those who had stood so proud a few moments before, made butcher's offal. Perhaps she should have felt triumph, but all she felt was terror.

> 'This is the end of the world,' she whispered. The end of the world she had known, anyway. *What had been strong was strong no longer.* What had been certain was wreathed in a fog of doubt. (Abercrombie 2015, 387 [my emphasis])

The horror evoked in this scene, in a text with no little amount of violence, stems precisely from the onrushing future, represented by the machine guns, and is directly tied to the body. The horrific future weapons reduce Viking warriors to "butcher's offal", stripping them of humanity even more thoroughly than Bayaz's disregard for his soldiers' lives, bringing with it the possible depletion of all that "had been strong" and "certain" – that is, the mighty Viking body and the way of the world predicated upon it.

The apparent antagonists of the series in *Half a King* are the High King and in particular his scheming advisor Grandmother Wexen, plotting to take over the North and convert the region – which was what, historically, eventually marked the end of the period of the Viking Age.[32] At the close of *Half a War*, the High King and Wexen have been supplanted not only by Skara, with Yarvi as "a slave [...] chained to his mistress", but also by other powerful women: Laithlin becomes queen-regent of Gettland after King Uthil's death, holding the throne for her three-year-old son, and Thorn leads her own raider crew, finally respected as a warrior and leader among men.

Much like in *The Red Queen's War*, the working class-connotated embodied power of the Viking exists not only in direct relation to institutional forms of power and other men, but also to empowered women and the changes in gender relations this comes to represent. In *The Shattered Sea*, the female characters seize power particularly through the successful mobilization of their female capital – recall for example Skara utilizing "her compassion", "generosity", and "mercy" in her encounter with Yarvi. The focus on this particular form of female empowerment – on women seizing power through superior competence, intellect, and ability to lead the more brutish and simpleminded men, being in control of their reproduction, and overall having the right to choose – can be understood in terms of a postfeminist formulation of female empowerment.

Here *postfeminism* refers to a popular contemporary feminist discourse focused on individualism, choice, and personal empowerment (Gill 2007, 149). It emerges in a neoliberal context, what Catherine Rottenberg defines

---

[32] Furthermore, in the appendix it is precisely the fact that Viking Age Scandinavia was "cut off from Christianity" that Abercrombie understands as fundamental to how "surprisingly tolerant" it was in regard to women (Abercrombie 2015a, 399).

as "not just as a set of economic policies but [...] a dominant political rationality that moves to and from the management of the state to the inner workings of the subject, recasting individuals as human capital and thus capital-enhancing agents [...] Everything is reduced to a market metrics [...]" (Banet-Weiser, Gill, and Rottenberg 2020, 8). Central to understanding postfeminist discourse in media representation, is how it simultaneously takes feminism and feminist critiques of traditional gender relations into account *and* repudiates it (McRobbie 2009, 12).

In research on masculinities in media, scholars on postfeminism have noted how men are represented as increasingly feeble and vulnerable, often in direct contrast to successful, empowered women. These portrayals may mock and undermine more conventional representations of male power, but as Gill writes: "In this way an unheroic construction of masculinity might be said to represent a *postfeminist modernization of hegemonic masculinity* that allows men to hold on to social power, while presenting them as harmless and troubled victims of a world where women rule" (Gill 2014, 201 [emphasis in original]; see also Gill and Hansen-Miller 2011).

Gill further links this unheroic masculinity to the uneasy depictions of the male body in this genre. Here the male body is a "site of anxiety" not because it fails to perform in masculine ways or because it is preoccupied with appearance in a typically feminine way, but because it emerges again and again as "hurting, vulnerable and anxious" (ibid., 196). Gill understands these portrayals as a way to construct and renegotiate masculinity and male power in a time of changing gender relations, where older models of traditional masculinity are no longer tenable, where feminist criticism of traditional forms of masculinity and male power is at once engaged and rebutted.

By comparison, the Viking hero is far from feeble or bodily vulnerable – quite the opposite. Even so, the Viking heroes (King Uthil, Gorm-gil-Grom, Brand, Raith, and, to some extent, Thorn) all become vulnerable to, in particular, female[33] control. Gill understands the construction of unheroic masculinity as a response to changes in gender relations in a postindustrial, neoliberal context – the decline of breadwinner masculinity in the face of an increasingly precarious, knowledge-based, and service-oriented job market next to gains in women's rights – that at once expresses this perceived vulnerability and implicitly repudiates feminist claims through the juxtaposition of successful women with failed men.

---

[33] Yarvi's position as a minister, a typically female role in this world, removes him as thoroughly from the category of 'man' as his hand: "I have sworn the Minister's Oath. I am not a man, in that sense" (Abercrombie 2015b, 156).

Viking men in *The Shattered Sea*, if considered as a representation of postfeminist masculinity, emerge not foremost as the "harmless [...] victims of a world where women rule", but rather as the *pawns* of more powerful women. The Viking men are at once unwitting bodies to be spent and offered, *and* a source of immense power to these women – it is as leaders of these powerful, physically strong men that these female characters are able to seize, and hold onto, power.

In other words, the brute physicality of the Viking body simultaneously *enables* him to become a pawn in these "webs" of power – recall that the action hero prevails through his body, and notably not through rationality (Tasker 1993, 5–6) – *and* remains the source of his worth. The Viking action hero is highly vulnerable to political manipulation, which here represents the invisible yet material conditions of regulatory power, to return to Sedlmayr – even as he also functions as its outside.

The Viking as a Fantasy of Sovereignty

In "Cutting Off the King's Head: The Self-Discipling Fantasy of Neoliberal Sovereignty" (2016), political scientist Peter Bloom attempts to account for the role of sovereignty within neoliberalism. Central to his argument is that neoliberal governance, defined as a shift from traditional state rule towards the self-disciplining of subjects in accordance with a 'rational' market logic (Bloom 2016, 9), does not do away with sovereignty, but rather incorporates it. Far from obsolete or an oxymoron within neoliberalism, Bloom argues that sovereignty persists as an "affective fantasy" for the self-discipling subject (ibid.). This affective fantasy helps "[grant] individuals a sense of 'sovereign' agency perceived to be lacking in their existence as 'agency-less' disciplinary subjects of neoliberalism" (ibid., 10).

Bloom continues by writing that "the perceived presence of sovereignty provides a sense of 'self' to neoliberalism, personalizing power and allowing it to 'make sense' as more than just a heterogeneous collection of regulative norms and social technologies" (ibid., 18). The affective fantasy of sovereignty works to uphold neoliberal governmentality through personifying and embodying power – that is, making sense of the heterogeneity of neoliberal regulatory power by tying it to specific powerful figures – and thus offers the imaginary possibility of individual sovereignty. In other words, this fantasy works both by personalizing power in charismatic figures – Bloom takes the self-made entrepreneur as an heroic figure who has made it 'on their own' and thus secured their own autonomy as example (ibid., 22) – and by upholding the illusion that personal autonomy and sovereignty outside the workings of neoliberal governance is achievable: "The fantasmatic presence of a sovereign [...] anchors identity to a ruler, who can either be embraced or challenged, this providing the co-ordinates for individuals to 'extend' into a sense of 'self' linked to desires to be a ruler or ruled [...]" (ibid., 28). For Bloom, sovereignty at once becomes the imaginary outside to neoliberalism and central in upholding it.

If considered as a fantasy of sovereignty, the masculine Viking body can be understood in a similar manner. It provides an outside to the operations of regulatory or institutional power through its embodied strength. At the same time, the Viking can be considered the ultimate neoliberal ideal: self-made and completely self-sufficient, continuously made vulnerable by institutional operations of power but always capable of, in some way, regaining their autonomy by virtue of their muscular might and hardiness.

Chapter 4: The Uses and Abuses of the Viking Body

In *Popular Vikings: Constructions of Viking Identity in Twentieth Century Britain* (1998), Alexandra Service, reading Viking romances, argues that the Viking romance hero offers dual reading pleasure – not only the identification with the powerful, impermeable Viking raider, but also as his victim: "To vicariously maraud with the Vikings allows one to escape the restrictions imposed by daily existence in society, while to be carried off by a […] Viking barbarian provides adventure, fulfilment, and freedom both from responsibility […] and from civilised, ordered existence" (Service 1998, 158). She continues: "[…] I believe that it is possible for both female and male audiences to identify with the excesses of the Vikings, and with the combinations of victimisation, release and empowerment that can be experienced by the Vikings' prey" (ibid.).

The barbarian Viking's association with sexual violence and rape is of course a long-standing motif (Aronstein 2011; Sigurdson 2014). In the romance genre, this possibility often becomes titillating, a play on victimization and empowerment. Service, drawing on Janice Radway's *Reading the Romance: Women, Patriarchy, and Popular Literature* (1984), understands this as offering certain forms of reader pleasure (see also Wilkins 2016). In the previous chapter, I discussed the fantasy Viking in relation to sovereignty and empowerment but, as Service notes, the barbarian Viking invites not only a fantasy of adventure, self-dependence, and freedom but also its mirror image: the prospect of victimization and helplessness. Where in Service's reading this duality of sovereignty and victimization is split accordingly between the Viking barbarian and his "prey", the question of power versus powerlessness seems less easily delineated in my material, as evident in the case of Vikings in relation to portrayals of female power in the previous chapter.

There I discussed power mainly in terms of class and gender, as well as in relation to the question of governance, showing how the idea of the physically superior Viking warrior emerges as a form of critique of power systems interpreted as institutionalized, ephemeral, and arbitrary. These systems are in turn connotated with a sort of feminized modernity (here defined in terms of a Foucauldian medieval/modern distinction) at odds with traditional forms of masculinity – constructed as reassuringly resolute and located in something physical, tangible, and therefore implicitly more legitimate.

Yvonne Tasker argues that the primacy of the masculine heroic body in the action film is something of a double-edged sword, balancing between the glorification of power as located in this body and the commodification or objectification of that same body. Even as the action-hero body seems to reify masculine power and superiority, it is also offered up for consumption and the threat of being reduced to a sexualized object (Tasker 1993; see also Neale 1993).

Mark Simpson also points to this in *Male Impersonators: Men Performing Masculinity* (1994), where he reads the homoeroticism and instability inherent in bodybuilding, the action film, the war film, and other forms of 1980s male-oriented mass culture. Where Tasker deals with what the action-hero and action film as spectacle means in terms of gender and power beyond only a reification of conservative masculinity, Simpson is interested in how these ostentatious displays of supposedly secure and infallible masculinity always also reveal themselves as performance, giving "an insight into the *flux* of masculinity right at the moment it is meant to solidify it in a display of exaggerated biological masculine attributes" (Simpson 1994, 30 [emphasis in original]).

Key to Tasker's and Simpson's readings are how these representations of ostensibly secure, heterosexual, "biological" masculinity always also open this body up to other forms of readings and gazes, and to becoming a multifaceted object of desire not only to its intended male straight audiences, but also to queer and female gazes. Tasker, furthermore, understands the action film as offering possibilities of fantasy and empowerment to audiences who lead restricted lives in some way or other, which is hardly exclusive to men (Tasker 1993, 127). This multiplicity is also what Service points to in her reading of Viking romances: inherent in the appeal of the popular Viking is the escape it offers "both from responsibility […] and from civilised, ordered existence", which Service ties to its association with the barbarian and the fact that he is a "creature of extremes" (Service 1998, 64) – that is, his extreme form of masculinity.

In this chapter, I bring together Tasker's and Simpson's considerations of the complex uses and erotics of the masculine hero body with Service's understanding of the Viking as entailing a story of simultaneous empower-ment and vulnerability or helplessness. Specifically, I consider how the Viking body emerges in the fantasy text, what meaning(s) it holds, and how it is related to the intertwined concepts of power, sexuality, and desire.

The Viking as an Object of Desire

Following Service, we begin with a return to Jalan and Snorri in Lawrence's *The Red Queen's War*, discussed in the previous analytical chapters. There, I read their relationship as juxtaposing very different forms of masculine power, which allowed for the display and glorification of the embodied power of the Viking. However, at the same time as the Viking seems to offer up the ultimate power fantasy – a form of masculinity that is wholly independent, sovereign, and supreme – it also offers the other side of the same equation: dependence and relationality.

In his text on the shift in the relation between male homosociality and homosexuality in contemporary US culture, Ron Becker argues contemporary close relations between men are enabled by "appropriat[ing] cultural codes connected to homosexual bonding as a means of acknowledging the possibilities of homosocial bonding", and, importantly, that it is now "effeminacy, rather than homosexuality" that presents "the most salient threat to male bonding" (Becker 2014, 236). In other words, physically and emotionally close relations between men are acceptable and encouraged as long as the boundaries of hetero- and homosexuality and gender remain firmly intact.

As I showed in chapter two, Jalan becomes increasingly symbolically feminized in the text – associated closely with typically female roles in the fantasy narrative, as well as made physically unsafe and the potential victim of sexual violence in the wild North – in ways that underscore Snorri's Viking masculinity. If the Viking represents the ultimate form of masculinity, then all other forms of masculinity can safely be made subordinate to and dependent on it.

Similarly, in *A Land Fit for Heroes*, among all the men that Ringil lusts after, it is the Viking that is constructed as his most secret, deep-held desire, even as his yearning is ultimately ineffective. Even in a magical dimension where all possible parallel realities and opportunities merge, a queer Egar never appears as a possibility (Morgan 2011, 169). The Viking at once invites queer desire, even as, through the immensity of its heterosexual masculinity, it seems to shut it down.

The extremity of the Viking masculinity is at once an idealized power fantasy and what makes the Viking an object of desire in the text. Subsequently, the neo-medieval landscape is not only an idealized past in which masculinity is empowered and impenetrable in opposition to feminine vulnerability (Kaufman 2016), but where masculinity can equal both dominance and dependence, mediated by the logic of homosocial hierarchy (see Sedgwick 1985, 45, 66).

Kim Wilkins, also reading Viking romances, argues that the Viking, because of its opposition to modernity and rationality, can in romance literature function as a "safe zone" for fantasizing about and navigating male sexual aggression and violence, because it is so far derived from the here and now to make it almost a paranormal figure (Wilkins 2016, 11). Similarly, we can understand the extreme masculinity and heterosexuality of the fantasy Viking as opening up queer potentialities *by virtue* of this immensity. The Viking body appears, furthermore, to be safely offered up not only as a spectacle or a glorification of masculine physicality, but also a sexual object, regardless of to whom it is desirable.

At the same time, as Tasker (1993) and Valerie Walkerdine (1999) both point to, the displaying and glorification of the heroic action body is always accompanied by fear of powerlessness, of being reduced *to* the body. This becomes particularly salient in Abercrombie's *The Shattered Sea*, where the empowerment and victimization of the Viking body go hand in hand when the mighty Viking warriors become both dupes and tools of mighty female characters seizing power through the ostensibly more intangible means of politics and economy (see chapter three). Unlike Service and Wilkins' material, where empowerment and victimization are divided along the lines of the Viking and his prey, these states are not mutually exclusive here; rather the fantasy Viking emerges as simultaneously immensely empowered and always at risk of exploitation and victimization.

"I feel something like a whore": Exploiting the Viking Body

To look closer at these entanglements of power and powerlessness and how it relates to embodiment and gender, I turn to Abercrombie's *Best Served Cold* (*The First Law* #4). Loosely inspired by Alexandre Dumas' *The Count of Monte Cristo* (1844), *Best Served Cold* is the story of Monza Murcatto, a mercenary captain who finds herself betrayed by her employer and his six closest men. Her brother is murdered, and she is left for dead, but survives and vows revenge. She puts together a team to kill all seven men implicated in the plot.

Among her recruits is Shivers, the secondary protagonist. He has left the cold North for southern Styria (the quasi-equivalent of the medieval Mediterranean in the *First Law* world) in the hope of moving away from his bloody past and becoming a better man. As for Snorri and West in chapter three, the trip south becomes a journey away from the freedoms of the, albeit violent, North towards (economic) exploitation and powerlessness.

Styria is described as a ruthless, cutthroat place devoid of honor, "sport[ing] thugs and cutpurses on every corner, if you can even get through their gates without being robbed by the authorities" (Abercrombie 2007, 55; cf Larrington 2015, 16). Shivers quickly regrets leaving the North for Styria:

> He remembered sitting warm by the fire in a good house in Uffrith, with a belly full of meat and a head full of dreams, talking to Vossula about the wondrous city of Talins. He remembered it with some bitterness, because it was the bloody *merchant*, with his dewy eyes and his honey tales of home, who'd talked him into this nightmare jaunt to Styria. (Abercrombie 2010, 35 [my emphasis])

It is telling that it is a "bloody merchant" and his "honey tales" that lures Shivers away from the North; it is precisely economic exploitation that becomes the pain problem for Shivers in the south. Where in the North he fought for honor, glory, and homosocial respect, Shivers in Styria instead fights for economic survival – in the employ of a woman, no less.

Like him, Monza is a ruthless warrior, but unlike him she is a mercenary and has spent her time fighting for a corrupt regent and swindling her clients out of money by staging mock fights. When Monza finds Shivers, he is starving in the streets and has no choice but to accept her offer of employment. This is symbolic not only of the juxtaposition of embodied versus institutional/economic power as discussed in chapter three, but also, importantly, a very direct reversal of gender relations.

Shivers and Monza develop a sexual relationship, which further cements this reversal. The first time they sleep together, he wakes to her tossing a few coins on his chest as "a fair price for last night", which he doesn't appreciate very much:

> 'You're paying me? [...] I feel something like a whore.' [...]

> 'So you'll kill a man for money, but you won't suck a cunt for it?' She snorted. 'There's morals for you. You want my advice? Take the five and stick to killing in the future. That you've got talent for'. (Abercrombie 2010, 106)

In this scene economic and sexual dominance becomes twinned. Furthermore, it symbolically compares Shivers being in Monza's employ with prostitution and shows Shivers' increasing discomfort with killing for money and what this arrangement may entail for his (bodily) autonomy.

This is closely tied to bodily comportment and what the Viking body is and is not supposedly for. He almost leaves Monza's employ when she murders one of the marks with an airborne poison, killing not only the man in questions but also dozens along with him. "Standing up and facing a man, that's one thing… but this–", Shiver protests (Abercrombie 2010, 111), appalled at the lack of masculine honor in using poison to dispatch one's enemies.[34] Monza has not only to offer him more money but also a promise that the incident will not be repeated for him to agree to stay in her employ.

At this point, however, his unease begins to manifest itself as bodily discomfort, distinctly connected to the geographical locations of the Styrian cities they travel through: "[…] lamps bobbing through the gloom as some revel wended into the night from tavern, to brothel, to gambling den, to smoke-house. Made Shivers' head spin, and left him sicker than ever. Felt like he'd been sick for weeks. Ever since Westport" (Abercrombie 2010, 118). Shivers' bodily disorientation is symbolized in relation to the seedy establishments lining their way into the city, linked to prostitution, economic irresponsibility, and general depravity. It also began in Westport, the place of the poison incident.

Furthermore, Shivers' financial vulnerability becomes closely tied to sexuality and objectification in the text. The second time he and Monza are described having sex,

> [s]he pushed her finger into his arsehole, up to the first knuckle.

> 'What the fuck?' He broke clear of her as if she'd slapped him in the face, stopped moving, still and tense above her. She jerked her left hand back, her left still busy between her legs.

> 'Alright,' she hissed. 'Doesn't make you any less of a man, you know. […]'

> 'Not that. D'you hear something?' (Abercrombie 2010, 232)

Catherine Waldby argues that the sexual configuration of the hegemonic male heterosexual body is constructed in terms of idealized "'imaginary anatomies'" (Waldby 1995, 268), which structure desire, pleasure, and sexuality along heteronormative lines, rather than actual anatomical comport-

---

[34] Compare this to Raith's symbolic exclusion from the male brotherhood from killing his king with poison hidden in a cup of wine discussed in chapter three.

ment. The imaginary anatomy of the heterosexual male body in this sense builds from its supposed impenetrability (ibid.). She writes: "The benefits for men of identification with a phallic imago derive from the kind of social power it confers, the various attributions of mastery it solicits from others" (ibid., 271).

Waldby is mainly concerned with undermining the conceptualization of the heterosexual male body as an impenetrable "war body" by asking what possibilities this might close down in terms of eroticism and pleasure. I here, on the other hand, am more interested in how the Viking emerges as almost a literalization of this "war body": sovereign, a destroyer, violent and impenetrable, always "armed and armoured". Waldby argues that moving beyond the supposed impenetrability of the male heterosexual body may open routes to alternate configurations of sexuality and power, but here I would argue that the association of sexual penetration with mastery remains intact – even as the possibility of the Viking war body enjoying getting fucked is definitely there, in Shivers' casual dismissal of being thought less of a man by being fingered (he did, after all, hear something; I return to that in the next section).

Kristen Barber and Tristan Bridges in "Marketing Manhood in a 'Post-Feminist' Age" (2017) argue that contemporary marketing makes use of hybrid masculinities to simultaneously uphold and mock traditional, hegemonic forms of masculinity. This is done by intentionally contrasting "intentionally excessive displays of masculinity" with feminine consumer protocols. This, they argue,

> offers viewers the appearance of something progressive by seemingly mocking or deriding configurations of masculinity that have sustained feminist criticism, including hetero-romantic and hard-bodied, action hero masculinities. These images offer a playful, ironic masculinity, and invite us to take pleasure in men who clearly embody idealized forms of masculinity while engaging in 'feminine' consumption practices. But this joke really only works if the systems of power are both carefully concealed and reinforced. (Barber and Bridges 2017, 43)

In the commercials Barber and Bridges examine, "hard-bodied, action hero masculinities" come across as either novel and progressive or undermined by being framed by feminine consumer or viewing protocols, which simultaneously display and downplay these forms of masculinities. Like how Rosalind Gill (2014) understands contemporary fiction that portrays modern men as fumbling losers next to powerfully adept women as obscuring gendered power relations, this 'softening' of representations of masculinities that have historically been interpreted as conservative and chauvinistic seems offer up a repudiation of problematic forms of masculinity even as they are rehabilitated and reproduced.

If action-hero masculinity has sustained a lot of feminist criticism, the same holds even more true for the popular Viking, which, as I discussed in the introduction, is often interpreted – not to mention intentionally used – as a symbol of white, male supremacy, intimately connected with Nazism, violence, and masculinist ideas about martial as well as sexual conquest.

Much like Barber and Bridges' material, irony and satire are hallmarks of gritty fantasy. Previous research on Abercrombie's work (Sedlmayr 2014; Petzold 2017), as well as other gritty fantasy texts (Carroll 2018), have generally understood this use of irony and satire as a critique of chivalric and heroic masculinities, revealing them as ultimately toxic. For example, like all the greatest Northman warriors, Shivers is a Named man, having received his name for remarkable deeds in battle. He claims he is called Shivers because his "enemies shiver with fear when they see [him]" – in reality he received the name after he, during his first skirmish, got drunk, fell into a river, and was shivering terribly once fished out (Abercrombie 2010, 473). In a way, Shivers perfectly encapsulates this deconstructive impulse in Abercrombie's texts: the mighty barbarian Viking warrior is introduced, and immediately humorously undermined.

Put next to the queer desirability of the male Viking body and to the postfeminist configurations of power in *The Shattered Sea*, where Viking warriors become both the tools and victims of strong women wielding political power (see chapter three) however, we can ask what else the reversal of Shivers and Monza's relationship, symbolized by economic exploitation as well as sexual dominance, may signify. Offering the Viking body up for queer enjoyment, hinting at its fuckability, and portraying it as subservient to women can be read as another form of postfeminist repudiation. The idealized hardbody masculinity of the Viking is undermined or painted as progressive by reframing its inherent heterosexism and impenetrability, thus rendering it safe from the same form of criticism.

Man or Meat? The Function and Form of the Male Body

As noted in the last section, Shivers does hear a noise outside the room, and in the next instant he and Monza has been arrested and brought before a torturer. Their arrest turns out to be a case of mistaken identity, but before they are released, Shivers has already been tortured:

> [...] Langrier stepped forwards and pressed the yellow-hot metal to Shivers' face. It made a sound like a slice of bacon dropped into a pan, but louder, and with his mindless, blubbering screech on top of it, of course. His back arched, his body thrashed and trembled like a fish on a line [...] Greasy steam shot up, a little gout of flame that Langrier blew out with a practiced puff of air through pursed lips, grinding the iron one way and then the other into his eye. [...]
>
> The room smelled of charred meat. (Abercrombie 2010, 244)

Even as Monza's sexual penetration of Shivers is aborted, it is replaced and concluded by a female torturer shoving a hot metal rod into his eye in an inverted mirroring of the preceding sex scene, making him "[thrash] and [tremble]" from pain rather than pleasure. If his "nightmare jaunt to Styria" has been a slow descent into dependency and exploitation, it is here that Shivers goes from man to "meat", wholly overpowered by the corrupt Styrian government, notably represented by a sadistic woman carrying out Shivers' mutilation with "practiced" efficiency.

It also proves the nihilistic conclusion to Shivers' attempts to become a better man. As Sedlmayr writes, the gritty fantasy never leads to change or restoration, but is rather characterized by a narrative cycle that eventually closes in on itself (Sedlmayr 2014, 176). Thus, Shivers' ambition to better himself is ultimately thwarted. At the close of the novel, he returns to the North, thinking that "he was a better man, of that he'd no doubt. A wiser man. Used to be he was his own worst enemy. Now he was everyone else's" (Abercrombie 2010, 534). Unlike Odin from Norse mythology who sacrificed one eye to gain wisdom, Shivers becoming a "wiser man" is not development and does not truly gain him deeper insight into the world – it just turns him more firmly into the man he left the North to escape in the first place.

In fact, he has only caught up with his own legend, truly becoming a man that people proverbially shiver at the sight of: "They looked at him first with mild disdain on their powdered faces, like he was made of rotting meat. Then, once he'd turned the left side of his face forward, with a sick horror that gave him three parts grim satisfaction and one part sick horror of his own" (Abercrombie 2010, 365). This scene takes place in a ballroom among the Styrian elite, next to whose beauty and finery Shivers stands out, both as a Northman and because of his mutilated face. Interestingly, he understands himself as "rotting meat" through their gazes even before they see his destroyed face, which he insists on showing off. As Tasker writes, the hardbody action hero always return to the question and fear of being reduced to a body, a constant tension between being man and being meat.

Steven Neale has argued that Laura Mulvey's classic demarcation between male characters as active subjects and female as passive objects in cinema to some extent breaks down in the action film, with the hero's body continuously halting the narrative to be shown off (Neale 1993). Paul Smith, however, criticizes what he sees as a too easy folding-together of different forms of eroticization (Smith 1995). Through a reading of Clint Eastwood's *oeuvre*, he argues that the eroticization of the male action-hero body is not reached through feminization of that body, but rather through different cinematic and narrative protocols, which instead achieve a *masculinizing* eroticization.

Following Paul Willemen's reading of the Western, Smith outlines three stages of the eroticization of the action hero: (1) the body is offered up as (erotic) spectacle, (2) followed by the destruction of that body, (3) followed in turn by that body emerging triumphant, restored through his own use of violence in the climax of the narrative (Smith 1995, 80–81). These three stages offer the male body up for viewing pleasure, even as they confirm and reproduce the masculinization of that body. Significant, however, is that the mutilation of the body cannot be taken too far; it is only "a *temporary* test of the male body", and the possibility of transcendence must be retained (ibid., 87 [emphasis in original]). According to Willeman, these stages all offer viewing pleasure: the initial display of the body invites admiration, while the mutilation, and subsequent triumph, offer up the thrill of the body in use (paraphrased in Smith 1995).

The potential objectification of the Viking body is an ever-present tension in these texts, from Jalan's humorous and envious appreciation of Snorri's body – described in impeccable detail throughout the three novels – to Ringil's repressed desire for Egar, and Monza's sexual-economic domination of Shivers. As Simpson points out, the queer potentiality of supposedly safe masculine pursuits like bodybuilding or war film lies partly in the framing of the male body and partly in its intense homosociality (Simpson 1994, 7).

In Abercrombie's *The Heroes* (*The First Law* #5), an ironic fantasy subversion of the war film, which takes place during a three-day battle and has an almost exclusively male cast of characters, the horror and intensity of the battlefield repeatedly borders on eroticism:

> *Even better than the sword.* [...] *More personal.* [...] No need for discussion or justification, for introductions or etiquette, for guilt or excuses. Only the incredible release of violence. So powerful that he felt that this golden-armoured man must be his best friend in all the world. *I love you. I love you, and that is why I must smash your head apart.* (Abercrombie 2011, 189 [emphasis in original])

> *The perfect moment.* Gorst knew nothing about this man, not even his name. *But we are still bound closer than lovers, because we share this one sublime splinter of time.* (ibid., 480 [emphasis in original])

At other times, the fight is compared to a "harvest dance" (ibid., 366) and the folding of a banner is likened to the care a bride might take with her "wedding shawl" (ibid., 501). Going back to what Barber and Bridges write about the use of satire and irony in postfeminist representations of hardbody masculinity, I wonder if this is not a tacit, tongue-in-cheek acknowledgement of the fact that, for all the supposed heterosexuality of these violent men, they are the gladdest and most comfortable pressed up against other men in the heat of battle, far away from women.

Smith writes that to further safeguard the eroticization of the heroic body against "possible disturbance in the field of sexuality", it is generally coupled with overt homophobia in the text, to clearly show for what purposes this body is displayed and not (Smith 1995, 85). Even as the ironic homoeroticism of this masculine environment is slyly pointed out, it is also further safeguarded against by recurring homophobic jokes about taking it up the ass (Abercrombie 2011, 20, 40, 412), as well as an almost anxious preoccupation with how disgusting two camps' worth of soldiers are, particularly focused on the digging of latrines and characters' stomach issues.[35] For all that the text invites the admiration and glorification of the heroic male body, it also paints it as ultimately revolting.

Returning to Shivers in *Best Served Cold* we can compare him to his antagonist foil, General Ganmark. Ganmark is one of the men Monza is out to kill, and like Shivers he came to Styria (from the Union) in search of better opportunities – thrown out of the Union army due to a "sexual indiscretion involving another officer", he went seeking a master who cared less about his

---

[35] In her reading of medievalism and *Pulp Fiction*, Carolyn Dinshaw argues that the reason John Travolta spends key scenes in the bathroom is to "reassure the (putatively straight) audience [...] that anuses *are* used for shitting" (Dinshaw 1999, 188) in an attempt to repudiate the queer potentiality in the film.

sexual proclivities than his "effective[ness]" in battle (Abercrombie 2010, 5–6).

Both he and Shivers are outsiders in their respective groups, and like Shivers he is presented as a peerless fighter, albeit of a vastly different caliber. Appearance-wise he is described as a man whose "face was strangely soft, his moustaches limp, his pale grey eyes always watery, lending him a look of perpetual sadness" (Abercrombie 2010, 5) – a noteworthy contrast to Shivers' scarred and brutal visage. He is a master swordsman well-schooled in the ways of military strategy who keeps quoting great old treatises on military tactics.

Shivers, by contrast, is described as being not "much of a reader" to the point of hardly being able to decipher a street sign (Abercrombie 2010, 20) and, in the way of the Viking, triumphs over his enemies more from the sheer force of his massive body and sword than honed skill. Unlike Shivers, Ganmark has no pretensions of becoming a better man; being an avid lover of art, he spends the aftermath of battles plundering for spoils and is shown to take more care to avoid damaging the prized artefacts he so covets than the men under his command.

Above all, Ganmark is a connoisseur of the male form. When Monza and Shivers find and ambush Ganmark he has just taken a manor on his regent's orders and stands admiring the spoils: "'Bonatine's Warrior.' Ganmark paced slowly towards it, smiling up at the looming marble image of Stolicus. 'Even more beautiful in person than by report. It shall look very well in the gardens of [my estate]'" (Abercrombie 2010, 270). The "marble" statue here evokes classical art as well as bodybuilding ideals, but like Simpson does in his queer reading of the bodybuilder's form, Ganmark insists on appreciating the heroic male body not foremost as a representation of strength and power or for its historic significance, but as an object, something primarily aesthetic, represented by his desire for men as well as his loving gaze upon the statue. Almost as a stand-in for the queer reader, Ganmark, by virtue of his sexuality and gaze, insists on interpreting Stolicus queerly, objectifying one of the greatest and manliest heroes and warriors of Union history.

During the ensuing fight, Ganmark is killed, not by Monza but by the statue itself, which suddenly topples:

> Ganmark was just about to turn as the point of Stolicus' giant sword pinned him between the shoulder blades, drove him to his knees, burst out through his stomach and crashed into the rock stones, spraying blood [...] The statue's legs broke apart as they hit the ground, noble feet left standing on the pedestal,

the rest cracking into muscular chunks and rolling around in a cloud of white marble dust. From the hips up, the proud image of the greatest soldier in history stayed in one magnificent piece, staring sternly down at [Ganmark], impaled on his monstrous sword beneath him. (Abercrombie 2010, 282)

There is plenty of Abercrombie's characteristic irony to be found in this scene, of course, in the fact that Ganmark is ultimately destroyed by the thing he thought he possessed. At the same time, it is hard not to read this scene – rife with imagery of sodomy and sexual subordination, Ganmark losing his life "impaled" on a "monstrous sword" – as a definitive excising, simultaneously, of the threat of homoeroticism represented by Ganmark's same-sex desire, the erotized heroic body as offered up as an aesthetic spectacle for consumption, *and* the objectifying gaze turned upon it.

This becomes especially pertinent when considered in the light of the juxtaposition with Shivers in this scene. It is at this point in the story that Shivers has just lost his eye, which has sent him into madness:

> Shivers wasn't himself. Or maybe he finally was […] [H]e was in hell. And he liked it. […]
>
> He smashed a sword away with his shield, tore it from a hand, was on the soldier behind it, arms around him, kissing his face, licking at him. He roared as he ran, ran, legs pounding, rammed him into one of the statues, sent it over, crashing into another, and another beyond that, tipping, smashing on the floor, breaking apart into chunks in a cloud of dust. […]
>
> A statue looked on disapproving.
>
> 'Look at me?' Shivers smashed its head off with his axe. Then he was on top of someone, not knowing how he got there, ramming the edge of his shield into a face until it was nothing but a shapeless mess of red. (Abercrombie 2010, 279–280)

Next to Ganmark's sexualized demise is Shivers "kissing" and "licking" at his opponents as he smashes the statues lining the corridor to pieces – statues which simultaneously evoke the possibility of the objectification of the male form *and* represent a threatening gaze on his own form.

Beside the aestheticization of the male body represented by the artwork and Ganmark's sexual and cultured appreciation, the Viking barbarian is all function and no form. If the mutilation of his face was not enough to turn Shivers from the potential object of Monza's gaze to a scarred warrior machine, the symbolic decapitation of the statue and safely smashing the enemy soldier into meat surely finishes the job. This is also the very moment Shivers finally gives up on his attempt to become a better man: "he was in hell. And he liked it." Supposedly a tragic (if not unexpected) turning point in Shivers' story, it is also a scene of spectacular, excessive violence, directly juxtaposed with the literal destruction of the very image of glorious, objectified heroism and male same-sex desire.

Unlike previous research on Abercrombie and gritty fantasy, I would argue that *Best Served Cold* less 'exposes' any horrors of heroic masculinity, than insists on the male heroic body as first and foremost *functional*, rather than aesthetic or sexualized. The violent destruction of Shivers' body, as well as Ganmark's gruesome death, at once rehabilitates or restores the action-hero body, making it safe from, and thus also paradoxically *for*, potentially (homo)erotic consumption.

Previous research on the action hero has pointed to its evident artificiality as well as inherent homoeroticism as sites of anxiousness in these portrayals (Tasker 1993; Simpson 1994; Fernbach 2000). This is also evident here, but I understand the emphasis on the underscoring of the functionality of the heroic Viking body as having further significance in this material.

At the close of the novel, Shivers has been imprisoned in Styria and watches as they build a gallows outside the window: "They had machines for planting crops, and machines for printing paper, and it seemed they had machines for killing folk too. Maybe that's what Morveer had meant when he spouted off about science, all those months ago" (Abercrombie 2010, 532). It is the final chapter, titled "Happy Endings", that includes this sardonic reflection about how progress apparently means more efficient ways of killing. In relation to Shivers, a killing machine himself and lately also employed in the business of killing, this holds no small manner of defeat: if machines can be used for killing in the future, what is the purpose of men like Shivers? Luckily, Shivers is released and free to return to the North, where "[b]eautiful men are even less well liked [...] than cowardly ones," as we learn in *The Heroes* (Abercrombie 2011, 24), the threatening future is yet kept at bay, and Shivers can still safely rely on this scarred Viking physique for a while yet.

This insistence on functionality, routed through homophobia and the reassuringly manly masculinity of the Viking body, can be put in relation to the negativity connotated with modernity and futurity as discussed in the previous chapter. Like Gill points to in her work on postfeminist masculinities (Gill 2014), the never-ending crisis in masculinity currently revolves around the supposed loss of traditional breadwinner masculinity, insecurity in the face of postindustrial societal shifts, as well as a more general question of men's roles and purpose in society (see also Kimmel 2017).

The sheer functionality of the masculine Viking body and the de(con)-struction of the sexualized male body here, can be understood as a way to insist on the male body (and, by extension, men) as something more than ornamental or decorative. This insistence seems furthermore to emerge directly in relation to both a felt loss of purpose of certain groups of men, as well as against feminist and queer readings of these forms of masculinity in media. The Viking here comes to signify both a reassuring return to a time where 'men were men' and a form of masculinity that can be salvaged and safeguarded from queer and feminist incursions into what is supposed to be evidently and securely male.

Interestingly enough, this salvage operation at the same time demands taking that same criticism into account, to return to Barber and Bridges (2017). For all the anxiousness regarding female sexual domination, male subservience, and homoeroticism to be found in these texts, they also to some extent acknowledge and depict these instabilities and possibilities. Even as the potential destruction and domination of the Viking heroic body are resolved and recuperated at the close of the text, this assuaging of masculine anxiety still hinges upon the *portrayal* of those same gendered anxieties, enabled and routed through the mighty Viking body.

The Viking Body as a Site of Exploration

I want to examine this further by turning to Elizabeth Bear and Sarah Monette's *The Iskryne Saga*. While somewhat different to the rest of the material, Bear and Monette's text also primarily works through a play on common fantasy tropes – as well as a feminist and queer reimagining of the Viking hero motif. Interestingly, the trilogy constitutes an intervention into the stereotypical, hypermasculine Viking hero image, even as it draws on the same figure of thought.

Conceived by the authors as an attempt to satire the 'animal-companion' subgenres of fantasy and romance, which generally anthropomorphizes and heterosexualizes human-animal relationships, *The Iskryne Saga* imagines a fantasy Viking age where men, telepathically bonded with gigantic wolves, live together in so-called "wolfhealls" to fight the trolls threatening the human villages of the North. Most of these men are described as outcasts in some way or other: "Disaffected men, younger sons, disgraced men. Men who practiced unmasculine arts – weaving, seithir – or some who were lovers of men" (Bear and Monette 2007, 17).

The wolfhalls are organized according to (fictionalized) wolfpack structures – including mating habits. When the wolves go into heat, so do their human "brothers" to some extent, and since all the wolf-bonded warriors are men, it means that while the male wolves mate with the female wolves, the men bonded to male wolves correspondingly have penetrative sex with the men bonded to female wolves. In short, Bear and Monette move the sexual coercion underlying most fantasy stories dealing with the 'animal-companion' subgenre – as well as romance stories more generally – away from the heterosexual couple/ing, through which it becomes naturalized and romanticized, to the abject activity of sex between men to make it visible.

While the larger plot of the story revolves around first the troll threat and later an invasion from the Rhean Empire (closely modelled on the real-world Roman Empire), the sexual politics of the wolfhalls is another major theme across the trilogy. The first novel in the series, *A Companion to Wolves* (2007), is about Isolfr who is brought to the wolfhall out of duty and eventually bonds with a female wolf. The wolfpack is led by one dominant female wolf and her male mate, and the men are led by these wolves' respective brothers, who become united in something akin to marriage. Unlike the majority of the "wolfcarls", as the wolf-bonded warriors are called, Isolfr has no desire for men and subsequently struggles greatly with what being bonded with a female wolf entails.

The Vikings in *The Iskryne Saga* follow the same general pattern as in the rest of the material: emerging in opposition to institutional power, portrayed as big, mighty, and primarily reliant on physical power, as well as stronger, tougher and manlier than most other men, and this contrast is achieved through the contrasting of the North with civilization.

So far, I have mainly discussed the Viking in relation to certain anxieties of masculinity and in regard to male power and changing gender relations in neoliberal Western society. *The Iskryne Saga* I instead understand as a text engaged with a rather different set of gendered anxieties, and read in relation to representations of female heroes, rather than male. It might seem essentializing to understand the male-authored texts as dealing primarily with 'male concerns', and the women-authored texts as dealing with some female equivalent. In my analysis I will show why I read the texts this way, but I would also like to note that while Bear and Monette's text is a fantasy, it also draws heavily on romance literature and fanfiction, genres that traditionally deal precisely with women's pleasures and concerns, especially in regard to autonomy, power, and sexuality (see Radway 1984; Popova 2018). I will mainly read the text as fantasy here, since it was published as fantasy and because, while incorporating romance elements, it does not follow a traditional romance narrative, but rather the typical heroic journey of fantasy. As discussed in the first section, Vikings have long been featured in romance texts and, according to both Service (1998) and Wilkins (2016), open up for certain possibilities in relation to concerns regarding empowerment and sexuality through the heroine's relation with a barbarian Viking. Bear and Monette use their Viking hero differently: the central narrative engine in their text is not a relationship, but rather an individual heroic journey.

In an analogue to the non-Viking characters of Jalan and Ladisla, Isolfr is closely aligned with women and women's roles in the text. As early as page four in *Companion to Wolves* (*The Iskryne Saga* #1), his father is told by the local wolfjarl that his son is a "[h]andsome lad. He takes after your lady wife [...]" (Bear and Monette 2007, 4). The novel opens with Isolfr being disowned by his father for agreeing to be tithed to the wolfhall, which requires a steady supply of new warriors to train every year. His mother sees him off alone, telling him that he must himself "decide what your honour is [...] and hold on to it" (Bear and Monette 2007, 11).

As Isolfr is taken up as part of the all-male warrior brotherhood of the wolfhall, he becomes increasingly feminized in the text. For example, as his wolf's first mating draws near, he is reached by news that is sister is engaged to a much older man Isolfr dislikes, and he both compares their respective situations and sympathizes with her plight because it reminds him of his own (Bear and Monette 2007, 178). Furthermore, while Othinn (Odin) is worshipped as the god of war and wolves, Isolfr himself is instead protected by Freya, something he is not particularly pleased by: "*Goddess of whores, how singularly appropriate* [...]" (Bear and Monette 2007, 245 [emphasis in original]).

Jane Tolmie argues in "Medievalism and the Fantasy Heroine" (2006) that female heroes in popular fantasy chiefly "have patriarchy itself as [their] adventure" (Tolmie 2006, 157). According to her, the most common and continuously recurring fantasy heroine is the strong, exceptional woman triumphantly and individually rising above a patriarchal system trying to keep her in place, which makes her a singular figure against a background of submissive women: "She often picks the man she wants, eludes the (many) others, escapes rape, lives a life less ordinary. Behind her and all around her is the silent rank and file of women who do not choose, elude, or escape" (ibid., 146). Tolmie cites historian Carol J. Clover's reading of strong women in the Icelandic Sagas, who argues that "that the real fantasy here is the dream of female autonomy" (ibid., 156).

In her article, Tolmie points to the recurring and rather narrow narrative within which the fantasy heroine exists; she becomes a hero by rebelling against a patriarchal system arguing that she does not have the right to engage in male activities, such as bearing arms, and that she is only fit for female roles like marriage, childbearing, and embroidery. However, while she ultimately gains her freedom or right to do as she pleases, hers is a singular victory that achieves nothing for any other woman in the text or affects any decisive change within the fantasy world.[36]

Just like the fantasy heroine, Isolfr has to struggle to be allowed to be a hero and warrior on the same premises as the rest of the wolfhall warriors, all the while being treated differently because of his female wolf, his role in the hall, and his beauty. Being bonded with a female wolf does not only mean that he has to "lay down" for other men, but also that he is responsible for the emotional well-being of the wolfhall. Furthermore, like the fantasy heroine, Isolfr bucks tradition and refuses his given path by choosing to become a warrior against his father's wishes. He is portrayed as exceptional through the way he makes a political alliance with the reclusive svartalfar, which helps them win the drawn-out war against the trolls once and for all.

Unlike the fantasy heroine, however, he ultimately comes up powerless against the thing that he finds most disempowering: being forced to bodily submit to the needs of the wolfhall. Like the fantasy heroine he must navigate societal constraints arising from biological difference, sexuality, and reproduction, but unlike her he never quite manages to rise above them. Instead, it is through enduring his circumstances that he is depicted as finding his own strength and a way to deal with them: "[H]e had chosen this; he had gone into it knowing what sacrifices might be demanded. And he had survived it" (Bear and Monette 2007, 187).

He does more than simply endure, though. When he discovers that not only the svartalfar but also the trolls live in matriarchal societies, he is enraged on behalf of both himself and of women generally. In the midst of battle, recognizing his troll opponent as a female warrior and smith, he

> thought of Thorlot, who might be a better smith than her father or brother or
> dead husband, or that her son would be, but who would never be anything

---

[36] This of course also relates to the typically static and timeless nature of the portal-quest fantasy, as described by Farah Mendlesohn in *Rhetorics of Fantasy* (2008) – see introduction for further discussion.

more than a wife, sister, daughter, mother. [...] he didn't know whether he was angry at his own kind for their blindness or angry at the trolls for making him see how blind they were.

The trolls and the svartalfar [...] and he killed the next three trolls in a black and causeless fury. (Bear and Monette 2007, 295)

Isolfr's story thus becomes not one of triumphing over the system – his stepping into the role of hero cannot ultimately save him from systemic and sexual subjugation – but rather one of resignation, not necessarily to the way things are, but to the fact that one cannot overcome them easily or on an individual basis.

At the close of the story, Isolfr has begun to affect change: first and foremost by sending his daughter to be apprenticed by the svartalfar to have her grow up in their matriarchal society and hopefully have different opportunities in life than she otherwise would have had. Isolfr, then, illustrates the limits of the traditional fantasy heroine as a feminist symbol, and offers an alternative; rather than overcoming the system that keeps him in place on an individual basis, he attempts to affect structural change for others.

His daughter Alfgyfa's story is told in the third and final book in the series, aptly titled *An Apprentice to Elves* (2015). Interestingly, she, too, follows the typical fantasy heroine role of the exceptional woman triumphing over the patriarchal system. Not allowed to become a wolfcarl due to her gender, despite having grown up in the wolfhall since her mother left her with Isolfr when she was just a few years old, she escapes her apprenticeship with the elves. Against the wishes of her father and conventions of her community, she eventually bonds with a wild wolfpack and ends up playing an instrumental role in winning the war against the invading Rheans.

Where the traditional fantasy heroine story as described by Tolmie is subverted in *A Companion to Wolves*, it is more or less precisely adhered to in *An Apprentice of Elves*. I would argue that it is noteworthy that it is Isolfr, and not Alfgyfa, who is cast in the role of the typical fantasy heroine, only to subvert the story by being shown to submit to subjugation, rather than rising above it.

According to Tolmie, this persistent story of the strong woman rising above the system on the strength of her own merits elicits strong mainstream *and* counter cultural or feminist pleasure. The fact that Bear and Monette pick this particular trope apart in *A Companion to Wolves*, via Isolfr, only to later conform to it with Alfgyfa, suggests that the subversion is to some extent *enabled* by the fact that it is routed through the male Viking body, a male hero, male same-sex sexuality, and male homosociality. Bear and Monette's use of the Viking motif functions as a kind of feminist appropriation, which simultaneously queers the Viking through the way he embodies and allows for the subversion of a typically female power fantasy.

One way to read it is as a gleeful de(con)struction of the heterosexist masculinity of the Viking motif; however, like in Abercrombie's text, the Viking motif also functions as an arena in which to play out certain gendered anxieties regarding bodily and sexual autonomy and power and subjugation. In other words, the hardbody masculinity of the Viking may be understood as a site of exploration for negotiations of gender, sexuality, power, and victimization. The mighty, white, and supposedly straight and impenetrable Viking body becomes, in *The Iskryne Saga*, a site to safely play out and examine feminist anxieties regarding biological determinism and bodily vulnerabilities. In Abercrombie's text, that same body functions in a similar way in relation to questions regarding male autonomy and power.

Service locates the Viking's subversive potential in its position as an adventurer and barbarian outsider – to be swept up by the Vikings (whether literally in the text or as a reader) is to be taken away from "responsibility [and] civilised, ordered existence" (Service 1998, 158). Here, following research on the imperviousness and vulnerability of the hardbody action-hero, I also understand the Viking body as central. The Viking emerges as the manliest of men, embodying whiteness in its purest form (Lundström and Teitelbaum 2017), a literalization of the stylization of idealized hegemonic masculine bodily comportment Waldby (1995) refers to as the "war body". I understand this extreme masculinity of the Viking body as enabling these discussions of gendered power and powerlessness because it is constructed as not 'weighted down' by gendered, sexualized, or racialized discourses of constraint, bodily vulnerability, subjection, and dependence.

Conclusion: Steel as the Answer?

"Steel is the answer", Viking King Uthil says in Joe Abercrombie's *Half the World*; "Steel must always be the answer". (Abercrombie 2015c, 16) What, then, is steel the answer to?

"Steel" in my interpretation here relates to both the weapons that the Viking wields, and the Viking body itself – strong, impenetrable, unbreakable. It connotates, furthermore, a working-class coded masculine body, bringing to mind both muscularity as an aesthetic ideal and the bodily labor that produces it. Central to this study has been to consider the popular Viking as representative not only of traditional manhood or a reactionary grab for male power, but also a particular representation of power more generally, routed through a particular form of masculine embodiment.

As Yvonne Tasker shows in her work on the action-hero body, this form of hardbody masculinity becomes a specific interlocutor for concerns of power and autonomy because it is culturally at once so masculine and powerful in all its muscularity – a kind of cultural shorthand for power – and at the same time vulnerable to other forms of power (Tasker 1993). To understand the appeal of the popular Viking in the present moment, I examined the recurring motif of the Viking in contemporary gritty fantasy literature, a subgenre intimately concerned with questions of power, masculinity, as well as male and institutional failure.

I approached the material via a queer reading and a queer-theoretical approach to masculinity and power. The queer-theoretical approach enabled an examination of the Viking that took its association with (specific forms of) masculinity as central, but not as given or foreclosing other possibilities or ways of reading. Furthermore, it allowed a sensitivity to aspects of not only power and gender, but also sexuality and embodiment in relation to the question of legitimization of masculine power through representations of a male, working-class coded body. Additionally, Tasker's (1993) analysis of spectacular masculinities in action-hero narratives as well as Peter Bloom's (2016) considerations of the affective fantasy of sovereignty in neoliberalism proved helpful tools in understanding what possibilities exactly this form of normative, muscular, hardbody masculinity may evoke.

I found that in the worldbuilding of gritty fantasy, the fantasy Viking emerges as a barbarian motif and a representation of spectacularly embodied masculinity. In the fantasy medievalist world of the texts, the Viking is situated in a Nordic landscape constructed as the savage periphery of the pseudo-medieval West, and fantasy civilization more generally. The fantasy North becomes at once dangerous, distant, *and* closely joined through construction of familiarity through whiteness, evident from an examination of the fantasy cartography in the material.

Understanding the fantasy text means understanding the close relation-ship between character and landscape. This division between the fantasy North and civilization in the texts mirrors what Tasker describes as the home and hell geography of the action narrative. Here, civilization is made out to be a hellish home in which the hero cannot function – instead it is the harsh, hellish wilderness, where his body can be at once put to use and shown off, that is constituted as home. In my material, this home and hell relationality activates questions of sexuality and gender which revolve intensely around the Viking body, as well as concerns of homoeroticism, power differences, failed or loser masculinities, and the ambivalent specter of female em-powerment.

In terms of relationality, I understand the function of the Viking as oppositional – emerging not only as different but also in direct juxtaposition to civilization, aristocracy, politics, economy, modernity, and institutional forms of power more generally. Where other characters and other parts of the fantasy world represent forms of power extending from inherited privilege, formal power structures, capital, politics, or outright manipulation, power in the North, and significantly for the Viking, extends from the muscular masculine body, and its physical endurance and capability for vio-lence. The Viking represents a firm, clearly delineated, individual, and concrete form of power – next to the abstract, imperceptible, and arbitrary power of for example the court, the economy, or political persuasion.

This juxtaposition is not only spatial, but also temporal: the Viking is firmly tied to the past and divorced from the present, while these other forms of power are instead congruent with futurity. This is in particular articulated in the homosocial relations between various male characters in the texts. Here, the Viking's empowerment and independence emerge in contrast to male characters associated with civilization or the medieval West, whom, to a greater degree, end up victimized as a consequence of their subjection to institutional systems of power, particularly a future-oriented budding capitalist system.

On that note, the Viking also emerges as morally superior in the text – highly interesting, considering that gritty fantasy has tended to be understood, and purported, to do away with the nostalgic moralism of post-Tolkienian fantasy. The Viking is an immensely violent figure, emerging from a harsh and warlike North, but it is also steadfastly honor-bound and cannot ultimately be bought or brought under economic sway. In the fantasy text, the Viking repeatedly emerges as an anti-capitalist figure in opposition to the places, settings, and characters I have read as symbolic of futurity and neoliberalism.

Looking at *The Shattered Sea* in particular, the temporal–symbolic division is also specifically gendered, with female characters, often regardless of geographical origin or location, deftly navigating and exploiting these more intangible, future-oriented forms of power. Whether the Viking men are left behind or desperately clinging to the past is left open to interpretation. As postfeminist perspectives on masculinity show (Gill 2014; Barber and Bridges 2017; see also Carroll 2011), male power is mediated not only through shows of strength, but also a complex interplay of vulnerability and powerlessness.

The evocation of the Viking as a figure of the past invests it with precisely a pre-modern, simplistic power as located in the strong body that can emerge as outside the regulatory power characteristic of neoliberal governmentality. However, *of the past* can also come to mean *left behind in the past* in the material: that is, at the same time representing anxieties and vulnerabilities in relation to the roles and places of men and traditional masculinities in contemporary society.

In terms of Amy Kaufman's concept of "muscular medievalism" (2016), this gendered temporality derives from the dichotomy of the fantasy of an empowered masculine past with a vulnerable feminine present, but in relation to the fantasy Viking, I understand this distinction as more complex. The figure of the mighty, impenetrable Viking next to not only modernity as such, but modernity in the form of these webs and gargantuan machineries of abstract and yet immovable power extending into the future, is significant here, and not wholly reducible this gendered dichotomy. Rather, we can understand the Viking as an affective fantasy of sovereignty within the fantasy text: self-made, representing power as embodied and individualized, as well as personalizing and making neoliberal governance tangible by appearing as outside or antithetical to those institutions most closely associated with these threatening forms of power in the worldbuilding.

The steely body of the Viking – scarred, wounded, mutilated, and exploited but never defeated or ultimately broken down – in various ways becomes a way through which to articulate anxieties or concerns regarding (felt) shifts in the constitution of male power. Simultaneously, it becomes the reassuring answer to those same concerns and anxieties; by the virtue of the immensity of the Viking's ostensibly obvious and given manliness, it also reiterates male power and safely locates it not in a patriarchal structure or system, but in the male body itself.

The Viking is ultimately a figure, or fantasy, of freedom, which is evident in my material as well as in previous research on the popular Viking (Service 1998, 158). Seemingly standing outside structural forms of power, dependent only upon himself and his immense bodily strength, the Viking represents a very particular form of freedom. It is a fantasy of the independent subject, unencumbered by relationality, taken to its outmost point, as well an idealized image of masculinity as ultimately self-dependent and strong – located, furthermore, in a past imagined to be, in some sense, freer and, above all, more amicable to men (Kaufman 2016).

However, as Tasker continuously shows in her analysis, the strongman hero body is always balancing between extreme empowerment and exploitation, victimization, and objectification. Particularly, as *A Companion to Wolves* and *Best Served Cold* show, the Viking in the text also becomes a site of exploration, enabling a safe space to play out questions of autonomy, consent, and (sexual) exploitation, with the powerful Viking body shown as intensely restricted, victimized, and abused.

As I see it, however, that safe space is provided *because* of the Viking as this fantasy of idealized masculine sovereignty. At the same time as the supposed impermeability of the Viking body is undermined, it is reinforced. The Viking body becomes a fantasy of sovereignty precisely through the way it simultaneously helps articulate *and* exorcise any threat against that same sovereignty. This is exemplified in how the Viking body becomes objectified and an object for both straight and queer desire in the text, with the texts both inviting and closing down queer appreciation of the Viking form. In terms of what ideas of masculinity, sexuality, power, and embodiment the popular Viking mobilize, the Viking here simultaneously represents a normative form of masculine embodiment focused on the strong, muscular body, even as it also emerges in relation to homosexuality, queerness, and both typically male and female vulnerability in relation to questions of power and agency.

In my analysis, I have highlighted the impermeability of the Viking body as a normative, supposedly heterosexual, white, and male body as central. At the same time, it also prompts the question of when, how, and for whom the normative, violent, white Viking body can be understood as comfortable, safe, or 'unmarked' by power differentials. As Sara Ahmed writes, the idea of whiteness being unmarked or its pervasiveness inconspicuous holds true only for white people; for non-white people, the ubiquitous presence of whiteness is immediately and perpetually visible and noticeable (Ahmed 2004).

Ultimately, the function of the Viking in the fantasy text is multifaceted. I read it as a critique of modernity and in particular late-stage capitalism, with the Viking standing in direct opposition to it and functioning as its outside. This is escapist in the way it reiterates an idea of the masculine body as wholly independent and self-sufficient, able to stand outside all forms of governance and subjugation.

At the same time, the relationality of the Viking in opposition to civilization also makes visible and meaningful systems of power that, by their nature, are diffuse and invisible (cf Bloom 2016). Even so, the Viking at the same time emerges as the perfect neoliberal subject – liberated, autonomous, and self-made, subject to nothing and no one. A central appeal of the Viking as a popular motif, I argue, is precisely this ability to be conceived as at once freely *outside* of systemic and ephemeral power and its disempowering effects, *and* also as its foremost ideal.

In research on narratives of masculinity crises and 'loser men', the usage of an idealized, working-class coded male body has generally been understood as a nostalgic marker for a supposedly lost order of (white) male empowerment (Messner and Montez de Oca 2005; Green and Madison 2013). I understand the masculinity of the popular Viking as not only a reactionary hope for a return to male supremacy, but a wider comment on and a pleasurable repository of power and empowerment. It is important to understand this form of hardbody masculinity as symbolic of power and powerlessness both specifically as relating to concerns and anxieties regarding contemporary men and masculinity, and generally as a response to an overall sense of insecurity and lack of agency.

The steel, then, stands as an answer to a growing sense of powerlessness, a fantasy of sovereignty and potency in response to the felt lack of control, relating both to the experience of male disempowerment in the current moment, and a wider societal sense of alienation in the late-stage capitalist neoliberal present.

References

Abercrombie, Joe. 2006. *The Blade Itself*. London: Gollancz.

———. 2007. *Before They Are Hanged*. London: Gollancz.

———. 2009. *Last Argument of Kings*. London: Gollancz.

———. 2010. *Best Served Cold*. London: Gollancz.

———. 2011. *The Heroes*. London: Gollancz.

———. 2013. *Red Country*. London: Gollancz.

———. 2015a. *Half a King*. London: Harper Voyager.

———. 2015b. *Half the World*. London: Harper Voyager.

———. 2015c. *Half a War*. London: Harper Voyager.

Ahmed, Sara. 2004. "Declarations of Whiteness: The Non-Performativity of Anti-Racism." *Borderlands E-Journal* 3 (2): n. p.

Alexander, Susan M. 2003. "Stylish Hard Bodies: Branded Masculinity in Men's Health Magazine." *Sociological Perspectives* 46 (4): 535–554.

Andersen, Lars Pynt, Dannie Kjeldgaard, Frank Lindberg, and Jacob Östberg. 2019. "Nordic Branding: An Odyssey into the Nordic Myth Market." In *Nordic Consumer Culture: State, Market and Consumers*, edited by Søren Askegaard and Jacob Östberg. E-book: Palgrave Macmillan Cham, 213–238.

Angell, Svein Ivar, and Eirinn Larsen. 2022. "Introduction: Reimagining the Nordic Pasts." *Scandinavian Journal of History* 47 (5): 589–599.

Aronstein, Susan. 2011. "When Civilization Was Less Civilized: Erik the Viking." In *The Vikings on Film: Essays on Depictions of the Nordic Middle Ages*, edited by Kevin J. Harty. Jefferson: McFarland & Company, 72–82.

Arvidsson, Stefan. 2007. *Draksjukan: Mytiska fantasier hos Tolkien, Wagner och de Vries*. Lund: Nordic Academic Press.

Attebery, Brian. 1992. *Strategies of Fantasy*. Bloomington and Indianapolis: Indiana University Press.

Balfe, Myles. 2004. "Incredible Geographies? Orientalism and Genre Fantasy." *Social & Cultural Geography* 5 (1): 75–90.

Banet-Weiser, Sarah, Rosalind Gill, and Catherine Rottenberg. 2020. "Postfeminism, Popular Feminism and Neoliberal Feminism? Sarah Banet-Weiser, Rosalind Gill and Catherine Rottenberg in Conversation." *Feminist Theory* 21 (1): 3–24.

Barber, Kristen, and Tristan Bridges. 2017. "Marketing Manhood in a 'Post-Feminist' Age." *Contexts* 16 (2): 38–43.

Bark Persson, Anna. 2022. "Notes Towards Gritty Fantasy Medievalism, Temporality, and Worldbuilding." *Fafnir: Nordic Journal of Science Fiction and Fantasy Research* 9 (2): 69–81.

Bear, Elizabeth, and Sarah Monette. 2007. *A Companion to Wolves.* New York: Tor.

———. 2011. *The Tempering of Men.* New York: Tor.

———. 2015. *An Apprentice to Elves.* New York: Tor.

Becker, Ron. 2014. "Becoming Bromosexual: Straight Men, Gay Men, and Male Bonding on U.S. TV." In *Reading the Bromance: Homosocial Relationships in Film and Television,* edited by Michael DeAngelis. Detroit: Wayne State University Press, 233–254.

Bennett, Lisa, and Kim Wilkins. 2019. "'Strange Companies': The Northman in Popular Historical Fiction." *Journal of Historical Fictions* 2 (1): 1–17.

Berggren, Kalle. 2014. "Sticky Masculinity: Post-Structuralism, Phenomenology and Subjectivity in Critical Studies on Men." *Men and Masculinities* 17 (3): 231–252.

Bersani, Leo. 1987. "Is the Rectum a Grave?" *October* 43: 197–222.

———. 1995. "Loving Men." In *Constructing Masculinity,* edited by Maurice Berger, Brian Wallis, and Simon Watson. New York and London: Routledge, 115–123.

Birkett, Tom, and Roderick Dale. 2019. *The Vikings Reimagined: Reception, Recovery, Engagement.* E-book: Medieval Institute Publications.

Björklund, Jenny, and Ann-Sofie Lönngren. 2020. "Now You See It, Now You Don't: Queer Reading Strategies, Swedish Literature, and Historical (In)Visibility." *Scandinavian Studies* 92 (2): 196–228.

Bloom, Peter. 2016. "Cutting Off the King's Head: The Self Disciplining Fantasy of Neoliberal Sovereignty." *New Formations: A Journal of Culture/Theory/Politics* 88: 8–29.

Bordo, Susan. 1999. *The Male Body: A New Look at Men in Public and in Private.* New York: Farrar, Straus and Giroux.

Bridges, Tristan, and C. J. Pascoe. 2014. "Hybrid Masculinities: New Directions in the Sociology of Men and Masculinities." *Sociology Compass* 8 (3): 246–258.

Browning, Christopher S. 2007. "Branding Nordicity: Models, Identity and the Decline of Exceptionalism." *Cooperation and Conflict* 42 (1): 27–51.

Butler, Judith. 2006. *Gender Trouble: Feminism and the Subversion of Identity.* New York: Routledge.

Campbell, Joseph. 2004/1949. *The Hero with a Thousand Faces.* Princeton and Oxford: Princeton University Press.

Carroll, Hamilton. 2011. *Affirmative Reaction: New Formations of White Masculinity.* Durham: Duke University Press.

Carroll, Shiloh. 2018. *Medievalism in A Song of Ice and Fire and Game of Thrones.* E-book: Boydell and Brewer Limited.

Cederlund, Carl Olof. 2011. "The Modern Myth of the Viking." *Journal of Maritime Archaeology* 6 (1): 5–35.

Christiansen, Niels Finn, and Klaus Petersen. 2001. "Preface." *Scandinavian Journal of History* 26 (3): 153–156.

Clay, Andreana. 2007. "'I Used to be Scared of the Dick': Queer Women of Color, Hip-Hop, and Black Masculinity." In *Home Girls Make Some Noise! Hip-Hop Feminism Anthology*, edited by Gwendolyn D. Pough, Elaine Richardson, Aisha Durham, Rachel Raimist. Monroe: Parker Publishing, 149–165.

Clifford-Napoleone, Amber R. 2015. *Queerness in Heavy Metal Music: Metal Bent*. New York: Routledge.

Connell, Raewyn. 2008. *Maskuliniteter*. Göteborg: Daidalos.

Creed, Barbara. 1987. "From Here to Modernity: Feminism and Postmodernism." *Screen* 28 (2): 47–68.

Csicsery-Ronay Jr., Istvan. 2008. *The Seven Beauties of Science Fiction*. Middletown: Wesleyan University Press.

Dahl, Ulrika, Marianne Liljeström, and Ulla Manns. 2016. *The Geopolitics of Nordic and Russian Gender Research 1975–2005*. Huddinge: Södertörn University.

Dale, Roderick. 2020. "From Barbarian to Brand: The Vikings as a Marketing Tool." In *The Vikings Reimagined: Reception, Recovery, Engagement*, edited by Tom Birkett and Roderick Dale. E-book: Medieval Institute Publications, 214–231.

Davidson, Peter. 2005. *The Idea of North*. London: Reaktion Books.

DeAngelis, Michael. 2014. "Introduction." In *Reading the Bromance: Homosocial Relationships in Film and Television*, edited by Michael DeAngelis. Detroit: Wayne State University Press, 1–26.

Dinshaw, Carolyn. 1999. *Getting Medieval: Sexualities and Communities, Pre- and Postmodern*. Durham and London: Duke University Press.

Doty, Alexander. 1993. *Making Things Perfectly Queer: Interpreting Mass Culture*. Minneapolis: University of Minnesota Press.

Eco, Umberto. 1995. *Faith in Fakes: Travels in Hyperreality*. London: Minerva.

Eilertsen, Lill. 2012. "Freedom Loving Northerners: Norwegian Independence as Narrated in Three National Museums." In *Great Narratives of the Past: Traditions and Revisions in National Museums Conference Proceedings from EuNaMus, European National Museums: Identity Politics, the Uses of the Past and the European Citizen, Paris 29 June–1 July & 25–26 November 2011*, edited by Dominique Poulot, Felicity Bodenstein, and José María Lanzarote Guiral. Linköping: Linköping University Electronic Press, 179–216.

Ekman, Stefan. 2013. *Here Be Dragons: Exploring Fantasy Maps and Settings*. Middletown: Wesleyan University Press.

Ekman, Stefan, and Audrey Isabel Taylor. 2016. "Notes Toward a Critical Approach to Worlds and World-Building." *Fafnir: Nordic Journal of Science Fiction and Fantasy Research* 3 (3): 7–18.

Elliot, Geoffrey B. 2015. "Moving Beyond Tolkien's Medievalism: Robin Hobb's Farseer and Tawny Man Trilogies." In *Fantasy and Science Fiction Medievalisms: From Isaac Asimov to Game of Thrones*, edited by Helen Young. Amherst: Cambria Press, 183–198.

Fernbach, Amanda. 2000. "The Fetishization of Maculinity in Science Fiction: The Cyborg and the Console Cowboy." *Science Fiction Studies* 27 (2): 234–255.

Fetterley, Judith. 1978. *The Resisting Reader: A Feminist Approach to American Fiction.* Bloomington: Indiana University Press.

Ford Burley, Richard. 2019. "Ambiguous Images: 'Vikingness,' North American White Nationalism and the Threat of Appropriation." In *Vikings and the Vikings: Essays on Televison's History Channel Series*, edited by Peter Hardwick and Kate Lister. E-book: McFarland & Company, 201–223.

Freeman, Elizabeth. 2010. *Time Binds: Queer Temporalities, Queer Histories.* Durham: Duke University Press.

Friðriksdóttir, Jóhanna Katrín. 2021. *Valkyria: Vikingatidens kvinnor.* Translated by Henrik Gundenäs. Göteborg: Daidalos.

Gardell, Mattias. 2003. *Gods of the Blood: The Pagan Revival and White Separatism.* Durham: Duke University Press.

Gill, Rosalind. 2007. "Postfeminist Media Culture: Elements of a Sensibility." *European Journal of Cultural Studies* 10 (2): 147–166.

———. 2014. "Powerful Women, Vulnerable Men and Postfeminist Masculinity in Men's Popular Fiction." *Gender and Language* 8 (2): 185–204.

Gill, Rosalind, and David Hansen-Miller. 2011. "'Lad Flicks': Discursive Reconstructions of Masculinity in Popular Film." In *Feminism at the Movies: Understanding Gender in Contemporary Popular Cinema*, edited by Hilary Radner and Rebecca Stringer. New York: Routledge, 36–50.

Glover, Cameron. 2017. "Was This Woman the Khaleesi of The Vikings?" *Refinery 29*, September 10, 2017. https://www.refinery29.com/en-gb/2017/09/171531/viking-female-hero-bj581-grave. Accessed 7 December 2022.

Gökarıksel, Banu, Christopher Neubert, and Sara Smith. 2019. "Demographic Fever Dreams: Fragile Masculinity and Population Politics in the Rise of the Global Right." *Signs* 44 (3): 561–587.

Gottzén, Lucas. 2015. "Kvinnomisshandlare och maskulinitetens monstruösa framtid." *Tidskrift för genusvetenskap* 36 (1–2): 7–27.

Gottzén, Lucas, and Rickard Jonsson. 2012. *Andra män: Maskulinitet, normskapande och jämställdhet.* Malmö: Gleerups.

Gottzén, Lucas, Ulf Mellström, and Tamara Shefer. 2020. *Routledge International Handbook of Masculinity Studies.* Abingdon, Oxon: Routledge.

Götz, Norbert. 2009. "'Blue-Eyed Angels' at the League of Nations: The Genevese Construction of Norden." In *Regional Cooperation and International Organizations: The Nordic Model in Transnational Alignment*, edited by Norbert Götz and Heidi Haggrén. London: Routledge, 25–46.

Green, Kyle, and Madison van Oort. 2013. "'We Wear No Pants': Selling the Crisis of Masculinity in the 2010 Super Bowl Commercials." *Signs* 38 (3): 695–719.

Greenblatt, Stephen. 1980. *Renaissance Self-Fashioning: From More to Shakespeare.* Chicago: University of Chicago Press.

Halberstam, Jack. 2011. "'The Killer in Me Is the Killer in You': Homosexuality and Fascism." In *The Queer Art of Failure*. Durham and London: Duke University Press, 147–172.

Halberstam, Judith. 1998. *Female Masculinity*. Durham: Duke University Press.

Haraway, Donna. 1988. "Situated Knowledges: The Science Question in Feminism and the Privilege of Partial Perspective." *Feminist Studies* 14 (3): 575–599.

———. 1991. *Simians, Cyborgs, and Women: The Reinvention of Nature*. London: Free Association Books.

———. 1997. *Modest_Witness@Second_Millennium.FemaleMan©_Meets_OncoMouse: Feminism and Technoscience*. New York: Routledge.

Hardwick, Peter, and Kate Lister, eds. 2019. *Vikings and the Vikings: Essays on Television's History Channel Series*. E-book: McFarland & Company.

Harty, Kevin J., ed. 2011. *The Vikings on Film: Essays on Depictions of the Nordic Middle Ages*. North Carolina: McFarland & Company.

Hedenstierna-Jonson, Charlotte, Anna Kjellström, Torun Zachrisson, Maja Krzewińska, Veronica Sobrado, Neil Price, Torsten Günther, Mattias Jakobsson, Anders Götherström, and Jan Storå. 2017. "A Female Viking Warrior Confirmed by Genomics." *American Journal of Physical Anthropology* 164 (4): 853–860.

Holmqvist, Sam. 2017. *Transformationer: 1800-talets svenska translitteratur genom Lasse-Maja, C. J. L. Almqvist och Aurora Ljungstedt*. Göteborg: Makadam förlag.

Hume, Kathryn. 1984. *Fantasy and Mimesis. Responses to Reality in Western Literature*. New York and London: Methuen.

———. 2004. "Medieval Romance and Science Fiction: The Anatomy of Resemblance." *The Journal of Popular Culture* 16 (1): 15–26.

Jalava, Marja, and Bo Stråth. 2017. "Scandinavia / Norden." In *European Regions and Boundaries: A Conceptual History*, edited by Diana Mishkova and Balázs Trencsényi. New York and Oxford: Berghahn Books, 36–56.

Jameson, Fredric. 2005. *Archaeologies of the Future: The Desire Called Utopia and Other Science Fictions*. London: Verso.

Jeffords, Susan. 1994. *Hard Bodies: Hollywood Masculinity in the Reagan Era*. New Brunswick: Rutgers University Press.

Jones, Diana Wynne. 2006. *The Tough Guide to Fantasyland*. New York: Firebird.

Karkulehto, Sanna. 2012. "Litteraturforskning och queerpolitisk läsning." In *Queera läsningar: Litteraturvetenskap möter queerteori*, edited by Katri Kivilaakso, Ann-Sofie Lönngren and Rita Paqvalén. Halmstad: Rosenlarv förlag, 18–41.

Kaufman, Amy. 2016. "Muscular Medievalism." *The Year's Work in Medievalism* 31: 56-66.

Kennedy, Helen. 2006. "Illegitimate, Monstrous and Out There: Female 'Quake' Players and Inappropriate Pleasures." In *Feminism in Popular Culture*, edited by Joanne Hollows and Rachel Moseley. Oxford: Berg, 183–202.

Kettunen, Pauli. 1999. "Review Essay: A Return to the Figure of the Free Nordic Peasant: Øystein Sorensen and Bo Stråth (Eds.): The Cultural Construction of Norden. (Scandinavian University Press, 1997)." *Acta Sociologica* 42 (3): 259–269.

Kimmel, Michael. 1987. "The Contemporary 'Crisis' of Masculinity in Historical Perspective." In *The Making of Masculinities: The New Men's Studies*, edited by Harry Brod. Boston: Allen & Unwin.

Kimmel, Michael. 2017. *Angry White Men: American Masculinity at the End of an Era*. New York: Nation Books.

Kimmel, Michael, Jeff Hearn, and Raewyn Connell. 2005. *Handbook of Studies on Men and Masculinities*. Thousand Oaks: Sage Publications.

Kivilaakso, Katri, Ann-Sofie Lönngren, and Rita Paqvalén. 2012. "Förord." In *Queera läsningar: Litteraturvetenskap möter queerteori*, edited by Katri Kivilaakso, Ann-Sofie Lönngren, and Rita Paqvalén. Halmstad: Rosenlarv förlag, 8–16.

Klinge, Mattie. 1984. "Aspects of the Nordic Self." *Daedalus* 113 (2): 257–277.

Koivunen, Anu. 2010. "Yes We Can? The Promise of Affect for Queer Scholarship." *lambda nordica* 15 (3–4): 40–64.

Kolodny, Annette. 2012. *In Search of First Contact: The Vikings of Vinland, the Peoples of the Dawnland, and the Anglo-American Anxiety of Discovery*. Durham: Duke University Press.

Lahti, Martti. 1998. "Dressing Up in Power." *Journal of Homosexuality* 35 (3–4): 185–205.

Langer, Jessica. 2008. "The Familiar and the Foreign: Playing (Post)Colonialism in World of Warcraft." In *Digital Culture, Play, and Identity. A World of Warcraft Reader*, edited by Hilde G. Corneliussen and Jill Walker Rettberg. Cambridge, Massachusetts, London: The MIT Press, 87–108.

Larrington, Carolyne. 2015. *Winter Is Coming: The Medieval World of Game of Thrones*. London: IB Tauris.

Lawrence, Mark. 2015a. *Prince of Fools*. London: Harper Voyager.

———. 2015b. *The Liar's Key*. New York: Ace.

———. 2016. *The Wheel of Osheim*. New York: Ace.

Lewis, Katherine J. 2019. "'What Does a Man Do?' Representing and Performing Masculinity." In *Vikings and the Vikings: Essays on Television's History Channel Series*, edited by Peter Hardwick and Kate Lister. E-book: McFarland & Company, 59–76.

Lihammer, Anna, and Ted Hesselbom. 2021. *Vikingen: En historia om 1800-talets manlighet*. Lund: Historisk media.

Lindgren Leavenworth, Maria. 2010. "Exotic Norths?: Representations of Northern Scandinavia in S. H. Kent's Within the Arctic Circle and Bayard Taylor's Northern Travel." *Nordlit* 26: 1–14.

Loftsdóttir, Kristín. 2015. "The Exotic North: Gender, Nation Branding and Post-Colonialism in Iceland." *NORA: Nordic Journal of Feminist and Gender Research* 23 (4): 246–260.

Loftsdóttir, Kristín, and Lars Jensen. 2012. *Whiteness and Postcolonialism in the Nordic Region: Exceptionalism, Migrant Others and National Identities*. London and New York: Routledge.

Loftsdóttir, Kristín, Katla Kjartansdóttir, and Katrín Anna Lund. 2017. "Trapped in Clichés: Masculinity, Films and Tourism in Iceland." *Gender, Place & Culture* 24 (9): 1225–1242.

Lönnroth, Lars. 2017. *Det germanska spåret*. Stockholm: Natur och Kultur.

Loponen, Mika. 2019. *The Semiospheres of Prejudice in the Fantastic Arts: The Inherited Racism of Irrealia and Their Translation*. Diss., University of Helsinki.

Lundström, Catrin, and Benjamin R. Teitelbaum. 2017. "Nordic Whiteness: An Introduction." *Scandinavian Studies* 89 (2): 151–158.

Manea, Irina-Maria. 2016. *Valhalla Rising: The Construction of Cultural Identity Through Norse Myth in Scandinavian and German Pagan Metal*. Diss., University of Bucharest.

Manns, Ulla. 2018. "Om synlighet och läsbarhet: Samkönad sexualitet och kvinnorörelsens historieskrivning." In *Den kvinnliga tvåsamhetens frirum: Kvinnopar i kvinnorörelsen 1890–1960*, edited by Eva Borgström and Hanna Markusson Winkvist. Stockholm: Appell förlag, 297–317, 348–351.

Marques, Diana. 2016. "The Haunted Forest of *A Song of Ice and Fire*: A Space of Otherness." *Fafnir: Nordic Journal of Science Fiction and Fantasy Research* 3 (3): 31–40.

McRobbie, Angela. 2009. *The Aftermath of Feminism: Gender, Culture and Social Change*. London: SAGE.

Mendlesohn, Farah. 2008. *Rhetorics of Fantasy*. Middletown: Wesleyan University Press.

Mendlesohn, Farah, and Edward James. 2009. *A Short History of Fantasy*. London: Middlesex University Press.

Messner, Michael A., and Jeffrey Montez de Oca. 2005. "The Male Consumer as Loser: Beer and Liquor Ads in Mega Sports Media Events." *Signs* 30 (3): 1879–1909.

Miéville, China. 2002. "Tolkien: Middle Earth Meets Middle England." *Socialist Review*, 2002. http://socialistreview.org.uk/259/tolkien-middle-earth-meets-middle-england. Accessed 7 December 2022.

Millett, Kate. 2012. *Sexualpolitiken*. Stockholm: Pocky.

Morgan, Richard. 2008. *The Steel Remains*. London: Gollancz.

———. 2011. *The Cold Commands*. London: Gollancz.

———. 2014. *The Dark Defiles*. London: Gollancz.

Neale, Steve. 1993. "Prologue: Masculinity as Spectacle. Reflections on Men and Mainstream Cinema." In *Screening the Male. Exploring Masculinities in Hollywood Cinema*, edited by Steven Cohan and Ina Rae Hark. London and New York: Routledge, 9–20.

Newby, Andrew G. 2013. "'One Valhalla of the Free': Scandinavia, Britain and Northern Identity in the Mid-Nineteenth Century." In *Communicating the North: Media Structures and Images in the Making of the Nordic Region*, edited by Jonas Harvard and Peter Stadius. New York: Routledge, 147–169.

Noble, Jean Bobby. 2004. *Masculinities without Men? Female Masculinity in Twentieth-Century Fictions*. Vancouver: University of British Columbia Press.

O'Neill, Nathalie. 2017. "Viking Skeleton's DNA Test Proves Historians Wrong." *New York Post*, September 8, 2017. https://nypost.com/2017/09/08/viking-skeletons-dna-test-proves-historians-wrong/. Accessed 7 December 2022.

Pearce, Lynne. 1997. *Feminism and the Politics of Reading*. London: Arnold.

Pearson, Wendy G., Veronica Hollinger, and Joan Gordon. 2008. *Queer Universes: Sexualities in Science Fiction*. Liverpool: Liverpool University Press.

Petzold, Jochen. 2017. "Constructing and Deconstructing the Fantasy Hero: Joe Abercrombie's 'First Law' Trilogy." In *Heroes and Heroism in British Fiction Since 1800*, edited by B. Korte and S. Lethbridge. E-book: Palgrave Macmillan, 135–150.

Polack, Gillian. 2015. "Grim and Grimdark." In *Fantasy and Science Fiction Medievalisms: From Isaac Asimov to A Game of Thrones*, edited by Helen Young. Amherst: Cambria Press, 77–96.

Popova, Milena. 2018. "'Dogfuck Rapeworld': Omegaverse Fanfiction as a Critical Tool in Analyzing the Impact of Social Power Structures on Intimate Relationships and Sexual Consent." *Porn Studies* 5 (2): 175–191.

Price, Neil. 2020. "My Vikings and Real Vikings: Drama, Documentary, and Historical Consultancy." In *The Vikings Reimagined: Reception, Recovery, Engagement*, edited by Tom Birkett and Roderick Dale. E-book: Medieval Institute Publications, 28–43.

Radway, Janice A. 1984. *Reading the Romance: Women, Patriarchy, and Popular Literature*. Chapel Hill and London: The University of North Carolina Press.

Roberts, Adam. 2000. *Science Fiction*. London and New York: Routledge.

———. 2014. *Get Started in: Writing Science Fiction and Fantasy*. John Murray Learning. E-book.

Roine, Hanna-Riikka. 2016. *Imaginative, Immersive and Interactive Engagements: The Rhetoric of Worldbuilding in Contemporary Speculative Fiction*. Tampere: Tampere University Press.

Rose, Hilary. 1994. *Love, Power and Knowledge: Towards a Feminist Transformation of the Sciences*. Cambridge: Polity.

Rosenström, Saga, and Barbora Žiačková. 2022. "The North Engendered: Mythologized Histories, Gender and the Finnish Perspective on the Imagined Viking-Nordic Ideal." In *Finnishness, Whiteness and Coloniality*, edited by Josephine Hoegaerts, Tuire Liimatainen, Laura Hekanaho, and Elizabeth Peterson. Helsinki: Helsinki University Press, 73–97.

Salter, Anastasia, and Bridget Blodgett. 2017. *Toxic Geek Masculinity in Media: Sexism, Trolling, and Identity Policing*. Cham, Switzerland: Palgrave Macmillan.

Sawyer, Peter. 1962. *The Viking Age*. London: Arnold.

Schnurbein, Stefanie von. 2016. *Norse Revival: Transformations of Germanic Neopaganism*. Leiden and Boston: Brill.

Schram, Kristinn. 2009. "The Wild Wild North: The Narrative Cultures of Image Construction in Media and Everyday Life." In *Images of the North: Histories - Identities - Ideas*, edited by Sverrir Jakobsson. Leiden: Brill, 249–260.

Sedgwick, Eve Kosofsky. 1985. *Between Men: English Literature and Male Homosocial Desire*. New York: Colombia University Press.

———. 1995. "Gosh, Boy George, You Must Be Awfully Secure in Your Masculinity!" In *Constructing Masculinity*, edited by Maurice Berger, Brian Wallis, and Simon Watson. New York and London: Routledge, 11–20.

———. 1997. "Paranoid Reading and Reparative Reading; or, You're So Paranoid, You Probably Think This Introduction Is About You." In *Novel Gazing: Queer Readings in Fiction*. Durham: Duke University Press, 1–37.

———. 2008. *Epistemology of the Closet*. Berkeley: University of California Press.

Sedlmayr, Gerold. 2014. "Fantastic Body Politics in Joe Abercrombie's The First Law Trilogy." In *Politics in Fantasy Media: Essays on Ideology and Gender in Fiction, Film, Television and Games*, edited by Gerold Sedlmayr and Nicole Waller. Jefferson, North Carolina: McFarland & Company, 165–178.

Sellheim, Nikolas P. 2019. "'The Rage of the Northmen': Extreme Metal and North-Motivated Violence." *Polar Record* 54: 339–348.

Service, Alexandra. 1998. *Popular Vikings. Constructions of Viking Identity in the Twentieth Century Britain*. Diss., University of York.

Shippey, T. A. 1982. *The Road to Middle-Earth*. London: Allen & Unwin.

Sigurdson, Erika Ruth. 2014. "Violence and Historical Authenticity: Rape (and Pillage) in Popular Viking Fiction." *Scandinavian Studies* 86 (3): 249–267.

Simpson, Mark. 1994. *Male Impersonators: Men Performing Masculinity*. New York: Routledge.

Smith, Paul. 1995. "Eastwood Bound." In *Constructing Masculinity*, edited by Maurice Berger, Brian Wallis, and Simon Watson. New York and London: Routledge, 77–97.

Stadius, Peter. 2001. *Southern Perspectives on the North: Legends, Stereotypes, Images and Models*. Gdańsk and Berlin: Wydawnictwo Uniwersytetu Gdańskiego.

Spracklen, Karl. 2020. *Metal Music and the Re-Imagining of Masculinity, Place, Race and Nation*. E-book: Emerald Publishing Limited.

Strang, Johan, Jani Marjanen, and Mary Hilson. 2020. "A Rhetorical Perspective on Nordicness: From Creating Unity to Exporting Models." In *Contesting Nordicness: From Scandinavianism to the Nordic Brand*, edited by Johan Strang, Jani Marjanen, and Mary Hilson. Berlin, Boston: De Gruyter Oldenbourg, 1–34.

Stråth, Bo, and Øystein Sørensen. 1997. *The Cultural Construction of Norden*. Oslo, Stockholm, Copenhagen, Boston, Oxford: Scandinavian University Press.

Sundmark, Björn. 2014. "Wayward Warriors: The Viking Motif in Swedish and English Children's Literature." *Children's Literature in Education* 45: 197–201.

Suvin, Darko, and Gerry Canavan. 2016. *Metamorphoses of Science Fiction: On the Poetics and History of a Literary Genre*. Bern: Peter Lang.

Svanberg, Fredrik. 2003. *Decolonizing the Viking Age 1*. Stockholm: Almqvist & Wiksell International. Acta Archaeologica Lundensia.

Tasker, Yvonne. 1993. *Spectacular Bodies: Gender, Genre and the Action Cinema*. London: Routledge.

Thomas, Calvin. 2002. "Reenfleshing the Bright Boys: Or, How Male Bodies Matter to Feminist Theory." In *Masculinity Studies and Feminist Theory: New Directions*, edited by Judith Kegan Gardiner. New York: Columbia University Press, 60–89.

Tlostanova, Madina V., and Walter D. Mignolo. 2006. "Theorizing from the Borders: Shifting to Geo- and Body-Politics of Knowledge." *European Journal of Social Theory* 9 (2): 205–221.

Tolkien, J. R. R. 1997. "On Fairy-Stories." In *The Monsters and the Critics and Other Essays*, edited by Christopher Tolkien. London: HarperCollins, 109–161.

Vagianos, Alana. 2017. "DNA Test Reveals Powerful Viking Warrior Was Actually a Woman." *Huffington Post*, September 11, 2017. https://www.huffpost.com/entry/dna-test-reveals-powerful-viking-warrior-was-actually-a woman_n_59b68b72e4b0b5e53 1078e5b. Accessed 7 December 2022.

Waldby, Catherine. 1995. "Destruction: Boundary Erotics and Refigurations of the Heterosexual Male Body." In *Sexy Bodies: The Strange Carnalities of Feminism*, edited by Elizabeth Grosz and Elspeth Probyn. London and New York: Routledge, 266–277.

Walkerdine, Valerie. 1999. "Video Replay: Families, Films and Fantasy." In *Feminist Film Theory: A Reader*, edited by Sue Thornham. Edinburgh: Edinburgh University Press, 180–195.

Walser, Robert. 1993. *Running with the Devil: Power, Gender, and Madness in Heavy Metal Music*. Hanover: University Press of New England.

Wawn, Andrew. 2000. *The Vikings and the Victorians: Inventing the Old North in 19th-Century Britain*. Cambridge: D.S. Brewer.

Weed, Elizabeth. 2012. "'The Way We Read Now.'" *History of the Present* 2 (1): 95–106.

Whitehead, Gudrun D. 2014. *Vikings, the Barbaric Heroes: Exploring the Viking Image in Museums in Iceland and England and Its Impact on Identity*. Diss., University of Leicester.

Whitehead, Stephen M. 2002. *Men and Masculinities: Key Themes and New Directions*. Cambridge and Malden: Polity Press.

Wiegman, Robyn. 2014. "The Times We're in: Queer Feminist Criticism and the Reparative 'Turn.'" *Feminist Theory* 15 (1): 4–25.

Wilkins, Kim. 2011. "'Cutting off the Head of the King': Sovereignty, Feudalism, Fantasy." *Australian Literary Studies* 26 (3–4): 133–146.

———. 2016. "'Ravished by Vikings': The Pre-Modern and the Paranormal in Viking Romance Fiction." *Journal of Popular Romance Studies*, n. p.

Williams, Howard M.R. 2016. "I Believe in Horned Helmets." *Archaeodeath. Death & Memory – Past & Present*. Blog. May 5, 2016. https://howardwilliamsblog.wordpress.com/2016/05/05/i-believe-in-horned-helmets/. Accessed 7 December 2022.

———. 2019. "Making Up Maketh Viking Warrior Women: An Archaeodeath Response Part 9." *Archaeodeath. Death & Memory – Past & Present*. Blog. January 11, 2019. https://howardwilliamsblog.wordpress.com/2019/01/11/making-up-maketh-viking-warrior-women-an-archaeodeath-response-part-9/. Accessed 7 December 2022.

Wolfe, Gary K. 2011. *Evaporating Genres: Essays on Fantastic Literature*. E-book: Wesleyan University Press.

Young, Helen. 2016. *Race and Popular Fantasy Literature: Habits of Whiteness*. New York: Routledge.

Young, Helen, and Kavita Mudan Finn. 2022. *Global Medievalism: An Introduction*. E-book: Cambridge University Press.

Žiačková, Barbora. 2019. "Imagining the (Modern) Viking." *ReNEW Third Nordic Challenges Conference*, 7–8 March, Copenhagen. Unpublished conference paper. Copenhagen Business School, 2019.

Österholm, Maria Margareta. 2012. *Ett flicklaboratorium i valda bitar: Skeva flickor i svenskspråkig prosa från 1980 till 2005*. Årsta: Rosenlarv förlag.

Summary

The aim of the dissertation was to study the Viking motif in contemporary Anglophone literature in relation to sexuality, masculinity, and power. The analysis emerged from three central research questions: What can a queer-theoretical reading of the popular Viking, focused on sexuality and embodiment, offer for understanding masculinity? What is the function of the Viking in the fantasy text? And finally: What ideas of masculinity, sexuality, power, and embodiment does the popular Viking mobilize?

Drawing on queer-theoretical perspectives on masculinity and the method of queer reading, I approached the Viking as at once bound up with the legitimization of normative and hegemonic forms of masculinity and open to (queer) negotiations and possibilities beyond normative male masculinities. Additional theoretical perspectives included feminist and queer scholarship on hardbody masculinities in media, postfeminist perspectives on masculinities, and Peter Bloom's notion of the affective fantasy of sovereignty within neoliberalism (2016). This has served to put the fantasy Viking in relation to contemporary discourses and concerns on masculinity – particularly the idea of a crisis in masculinity – while also attempting to move beyond a direct and automatic connection between Viking masculinity and men or men's concerns and discuss Viking masculinity and embodiment in relation to power in a broader sense.

The empirical material consists of 18 fantasy texts across five authors (with two writing as a pair) drawn from the subgenre of gritty fantasy. Gritty fantasy as a subgenre of epic fantasy first emerged in the early 2000s. It is heavily invested in nihilism, disillusionment and contemporary concerns regarding masculinity, masculine failure, and masculinity crisis narratives, and here the Viking motif plays a major role. The texts under consideration are Joe Abercrombie's *The First Law* (2006–2012) and *The Shattered Sea* (2014–2015), Richard K. Morgan's *A Land Fit for Heroes* (2008–2016), Mark Lawrence's *The Red Queen's War* (2014–2016), and Elizabeth Bear and Sarah Monette's *The Iskryne Saga* (2007–2015).

Three chapters make up the analytical part of the dissertation. The first, "Into the Fantasy North", takes its starting point in fantasy worldbuilding and fantasy cartography. Previous research has shown that in genre fantasy there tends to be a close relationship between land and characters, and here I mapped out the relationship between the fantasy world, the North, and the Viking. Fantasy worlds furthermore tend to draw on pseudo-medieval conventions, reflecting and reproducing Eurocentric and colonial constructions of the world.

I found that in the worldbuilding of gritty fantasy, the fantasy Viking emerges as a barbarian motif and a representation of spectacularly embodied masculinity. In the fantasy medievalist world of the texts, the Viking is situated in a Nordic landscape constructed as the savage periphery of the pseudo-medieval West and fantasy civilization more generally. The fantasy North becomes at once dangerous, distant, *and* closely joined through a construction of familiarity through whiteness.

In the second analytical chapter, "No Future for Vikings – Temporality and Homosociality", I read the Viking and its homosocial relationships in relation to power and agency. I understand the Viking as an oppositional figure, emerging in direct juxtaposition to civilization, aristocracy, politics, economy, modernity, and institutional forms of power more generally. In the texts, other characters and other parts of the fantasy world represent forms of power extending from inherited privilege, formal power structures, capital, politics, or outright manipulation. By comparison, power in the North, and significantly for the Viking, extends from the muscular masculine body, and its physical endurance and capability for violence.

Importantly, the Viking represents a firm, clearly delineated, individual, and concrete form of power – next to the abstract, imperceptible, and arbitrary power of, for example, the court, the economy, or politics. In the material, the centrality of the Viking as a physically strong body, whose main recourse is that same body is key in the construction of the Viking as simultaneously impervious to and outside these forms of institutional power.

Furthermore, the fantasy Viking becomes meaningful not only in relation to spatiality, but also temporality. The Viking is firmly tied to the past and divorced from the present, while other forms of power, outlined above, are instead congruent with futurity. This is in particular articulated in homosocial relations between male characters. Here, the Viking's empowerment and independence emerge in contrast to male characters associated with civilization or the medieval West, whom to a greater degree end up victimized as a consequence of their subjection to institutional systems of power, particularly a future-oriented budding capitalist system.

This temporality is also highly gendered, with female characters, regardless of geographical origin or location, deftly navigating and exploiting these more intangible, future-oriented forms of power. The evocation of the Viking as a figure of the past invests it with precisely a pre-modern, simplistic power as located in the strong body that can emerge as outside the regulatory power characteristic of neoliberal governmentality. However, *of the past* can also come to mean *left behind in the past* in the texts; that is, at the same time representing anxieties and vulnerabilities in relation to the roles and places of men and traditional masculinities in contemporary society.

The final analytical chapter, "The Uses and Abuses of the Viking Body", looks more closely at Viking embodiment in the texts. In particular, it considers the Viking body as simultaneously a source of immense power and strength, while also objectified and with the Viking always threatened to be reduced to a mere body. Furthermore, the Viking body is intensely engaged in negotiations around (queer) desire and objectification, with the texts often insisting on the function of the Viking body above its form. At the same time, this ferocious and strong body also becomes a place to project discussions and concerns regarding embodiment, sexuality, agency, and disempowerment, in both masculinist and feminist terms.

The study shows that the fantasy Viking, as a subset of the popular Viking, can be considered a site where complex negotiations regarding the considerations of gender, power, and ideals of freedom emerge, tied into the idea of the Viking as shorthand for legitimate, normative, white, heterosexual, strongman masculinity. In one sense, the Viking does reflect and reproduce ideas of normative and dominant forms of masculinity, functioning as an image of idealized manhood. At the same time, precisely because it represents this form of impervious, epitomized form of masculinity – manly, mighty, white, supposedly straight – it also becomes symbolic of discussions of empowerment and disempowerment in ways that cannot be reducible solely to concerns relating to male masculinity and power.

I read the fantasy Viking in relation to the gritty medievalist fantasy world always moving inexorably towards an undesirable future as both making meaningful and, in some sense, visible the dissemination and invincibility/invisibility of neoliberal disciplinary power. At the same time, however, it offers a fantasy of empowerment, where it is possible to stand outside these discipling effects by the strength of one own's body and honor, effectively turning the Viking into the ultimate self-made subject. Wholly independent, strong, and self-sufficient while also supposedly outside all disciplinary operations of power.

I understand the masculinity of the popular Viking as not only a reactionary hope for a return to male supremacy, but a wider comment on and pleasurable repository of power and empowerment. In this way it relates *both* to concerns and anxieties specific to men and male masculinity in the current moment and to a more universal sense of insecurity and lack of agency.

The title of the dissertation asks what the steel – here connoting at once the impenetrable body of the Viking and the steel he wields – is the answer to. The response to that question, as found in the analysis, is that the steel stands as an answer foremost to a growing sense of powerlessness, a fantasy of sovereignty and potency in response to the felt lack of control, relating both to the experience of male disempowerment in the current moment and a wider societal sense of alienation in the late-stage capitalist neoliberal now.

Sammanfattning (Summary in Swedish)

Den här avhandlingen undersöker vikingamotivet i samtida engelskspråkig fantasylitteratur med fokus på maskulinitet, makt, kroppslighet och sexualitet. Studien tar avstamp i queerteoretiska perspektiv på maskulinitet och queer läsning som metod och förstår vikingen som på samma gång direkt kopplad till idéer om legitimering av normativa och hegemoniska former av maskulinitet och öppen för (queera) omförhandlingar och möjligheter bortom normativa manliga maskuliniteter.

Empiriskt utgår avhandlingen från en relativt ny subgenre av fantasy, gritty fantasy, som är djupt sammankopplad med samtida diskussioner kring maskulinitet i relation till misslyckande och kris och där vikingamotivet ofta har en framskjuten roll. Texterna som avhandlas är Joe Abercrombies *The First Law* (2006–2012) och *The Shattered Sea* (2014–2015), Richard K. Morgans *A Land Fit for Heroes* (2008–2016), Mark Lawrences *The Red Queen's War* (2014–2016) samt Elizabeth Bear och Sarah Monettes *The Iskryne Saga* (2007–2015).

Vikingen framträder som ett motiv som är djupt sammanbundet med idéer om det förflutna och historia, men som inte enbart kan reduceras till det. I stället förstår avhandlingen vikingen som en medial representation av spektakulär, kroppslig actionmaskulinitet och sätter den i relation till fantasytexten och fantasyvärldsbygget samt mer generella idéer om Norden. Vidare har den maskulina vikingen länge symboliskt kopplats ihop med reaktionära idéer om vit överhöghet, misogyni och homofobi, och avhandlingen intresserar sig för hur vikingens maskulinitet kan förstås bortom något som enbart förhåller sig till män eller mäns angelägenheter.

Studien diskuterar vikingen i relation till rumslighet, temporalitet och kroppslighet och finner att i fantasytexten skildras vikingen med en fokus på en stark, muskulös kropp och som en barbarisk Andra från det förflutna, i opposition till såväl civilisation som modernitet och framtid. Här positioneras vikingen som en eskapistisk möjlighet utanför och i motsats till det nyliberala, senkapitalistiska samhället och disciplinär makt. Vidare, via postfeministiska perspektiv på maskulinitet, finner avhandlingen att fantasyvikingen också verkar svara mot feministisk och queer kritik av traditionella och homofoba former av maskulinitet genom att omforma vikingen och positionera den som ett objekt för olika former av (queera) begär. Samtidigt blir vikingen också en symbolisk tillflykt för konservativa idéer om maskulinitet, där ängslan över en förmodad förlust av traditionellt manliga egenskaper och manlig makt i senmoderniteten kan projiceras och upplösas.

Nyckelord: vikingar, Norden, maskulinitet, fantasylitteratur, queer läsning, temporalitet, postfeminism, kroppslighet

Södertörn Doctoral Dissertations

1. Jolanta Aidukaite, *The Emergence of the Post-Socialist Welfare State: The case of the Baltic States: Estonia, Latvia and Lithuania*, 2004

2. Xavier Fraudet, *Politique étrangère française en mer Baltique (1871–1914): de l'exclusion à l'affirmation*, 2005

3. Piotr Wawrzeniuk, *Confessional Civilising in Ukraine: The Bishop Iosyf Shumliansky and the Introduction of Reforms in the Diocese of Lviv 1668–1708*, 2005

4. Andrej Kotljarchuk, *In the Shadows of Poland and Russia: The Grand Duchy of Lithuania and Sweden in the European Crisis of the mid-17th Century*, 2006

5. Håkan Blomqvist, *Nation, ras och civilisation i svensk arbetarrörelse före nazismen*, 2006

6. Karin S Lindelöf, *Om vi nu ska bli som Europa: Könsskapande och normalitet bland unga kvinnor i transitionens Polen*, 2006

7. Andrew Stickley. *On Interpersonal Violence in Russia in the Present and the Past: A Sociological Study*, 2006

8. Arne Ek, *Att konstruera en uppslutning kring den enda vägen: Om folkrörelsers modernisering i skuggan av det Östeuropeiska systemskiftet*, 2006

9. Agnes Ers, *I mänsklighetens namn: En etnologisk studie av ett svenskt biståndsprojekt i Rumänien*, 2006

10. Johnny Rodin, *Rethinking Russian Federalism: The Politics of Intergovernmental Relations and Federal Reforms at the Turn of the Millennium*, 2006

11. Kristian Petrov, *Tillbaka till framtiden: Modernitet, postmodernitet och generationsidentitet i Gorbačevs glasnost' och perestrojka*, 2006

12. Sophie Söderholm Werkö, *Patient patients? Achieving Patient Empowerment through Active Participation, Increased Knowledge and Organisation*, 2008

13. Peter Bötker, *Leviatan i arkipelagen: Staten, förvaltningen och samhället. Fallet Estland*, 2007

14. Matilda Dahl, *States under scrutiny: International organizations, transformation and the construction of progress*, 2007

15. Margrethe B. Søvik, *Support, resistance and pragmatism: An examination of motivation in language policy in Kharkiv, Ukraine*, 2007

16. Yulia Gradskova, *Soviet People with female Bodies: Performing beauty and maternity in Soviet Russia in the mid 1930–1960s*, 2007

17. Renata Ingbrant, *From Her Point of View: Woman's Anti-World in the Poetry of Anna Świrszczyńska*, 2007

18. Johan Eellend, *Cultivating the Rural Citizen: Modernity, Agrarianism and Citizenship in Late Tsarist Estonia*, 2007

19. Petra Garberding, *Musik och politik i skuggan av nazismen: Kurt Atterberg och de svensk-tyska musikrelationerna*, 2007

20. Aleksei Semenenko, *Hamlet the Sign: Russian Translations of Hamlet and Literary Canon Formation*, 2007

21. Vytautas Petronis, *Constructing Lithuania: Ethnic Mapping in the Tsarist Russia, ca. 1800–1914*, 2007

22. Akvile Motiejunaite, *Female employment, gender roles, and attitudes: The Baltic countries in a broader context*, 2008

23. Tove Lindén, *Explaining Civil Society Core Activism in Post-Soviet Latvia*, 2008

24. Pelle Åberg, *Translating Popular Education: Civil Society Cooperation between Sweden and Estonia*, 2008

25. Anders Nordström, *The Interactive Dynamics of Regulation: Exploring the Council of Europe's monitoring of Ukraine*, 2008

26. Fredrik Doeser, *In Search of Security After the Collapse of the Soviet Union: Foreign Policy Change in Denmark, Finland and Sweden, 1988–1993*, 2008

27. Zhanna Kravchenko. *Family (versus) Policy: Combining Work and Care in Russia and Sweden*, 2008

28. Rein Jüriado, *Learning within and between public-private partnerships*, 2008

29. Elin Boalt, *Ecology and evolution of tolerance in two cruciferous species*, 2008

30. Lars Forsberg, *Genetic Aspects of Sexual Selection and Mate Choice in Salmonids*, 2008

31. Eglė Rindzevičiūtė, *Constructing Soviet Cultural Policy: Cybernetics and Governance in Lithuania after World War II*, 2008

32. Joakim Philipson, *The Purpose of Evolution: 'struggle for existence' in the Russian-Jewish press 1860–1900*, 2008

33. Sofie Bedford, *Islamic activism in Azerbaijan: Repression and mobilization in a post-Soviet context*, 2009

34. Tommy Larsson Segerlind, *Team Entrepreneurship: A process analysis of the venture team and the venture team roles in relation to the innovation process*, 2009

35. Jenny Svensson, *The Regulation of Rule-Following: Imitation and Soft Regulation in the European Union*, 2009

36. Stefan Hallgren, *Brain Aromatase in the guppy, Poecilia reticulate: Distribution, control and role in behavior*, 2009

37. Karin Ellencrona, *Functional characterization of interactions between the flavivirus NS5 protein and PDZ proteins of the mammalian host*, 2009

38. Makiko Kanematsu, *Saga och verklighet: Barnboksproduktion i det postsovjetiska Lettland*, 2009

39. Daniel Lindvall, *The Limits of the European Vision in Bosnia and Herzegovina: An Analysis of the Police Reform Negotiations*, 2009

40. Charlotta Hillerdal, *People in Between – Ethnicity and Material Identity: A New Approach to Deconstructed Concepts*, 2009

41. Jonna Bornemark, *Kunskapens gräns – gränsens vetande*, 2009

42. Adolphine G. Kateka, *Co-Management Challenges in the Lake Victoria Fisheries: A Context Approach*, 2010

43. René León Rosales, *Vid framtidens hitersta gräns: Om pojkar och elevpositioner i en multietnisk skola*, 2010

44. Simon Larsson, *Intelligensaristokrater och arkivmartyrer: Normerna för vetenskaplig skicklighet i svensk historieforskning 1900–1945*, 2010

45. Håkan Lättman, *Studies on spatial and temporal distributions of epiphytic lichens*, 2010

46. Alia Jaensson, *Pheromonal mediated behaviour and endocrine response in salmonids: The impact of cypermethrin, copper, and glyphosate*, 2010

47. Michael Wigerius, *Roles of mammalian Scribble in polarity signaling, virus offense and cell-fate determination*, 2010

48. Anna Hedtjärn Wester, *Män i kostym: Prinsar, konstnärer och tegelbärare vid sekelskiftet 1900*, 2010

49. Magnus Linnarsson, *Postgång på växlande villkor: Det svenska postväsendets organisation under stormaktstiden*, 2010

50. Barbara Kunz, *Kind words, cruise missiles and everything in between: A neoclassical realist study of the use of power resources in U.S. policies towards Poland, Ukraine and Belarus 1989–2008*, 2010

51. Anders Bartonek, *Philosophie im Konjunktiv: Nichtidentität als Ort der Möglichkeit des Utopischen in der negativen Dialektik Theodor W. Adornos*, 2010

52. Carl Cederberg, *Resaying the Human: Levinas Beyond Humanism and Antihumanism*, 2010

53. Johanna Ringarp, *Professionens problematik: Lärarkårens kommunalisering och välfärdsstatens förvandling*, 2011

54. Sofi Gerber, *Öst är Väst men Väst är bäst: Östtysk identitetsformering i det förenade Tyskland*, 2011

55. Susanna Sjödin Lindenskoug, *Manlighetens bortre gräns: Tidelagsrättegångar i Livland åren 1685–1709*, 2011

56. Dominika Polanska, *The emergence of enclaves of wealth and poverty: A sociological study of residential differentiation in post-communist Poland*, 2011

57. Christina Douglas, *Kärlek per korrespondens: Två förlovade par under andra hälften av 1800-talet*, 2011

58. Fred Saunders, *The Politics of People – Not just Mangroves and Monkeys: A study of the theory and practice of community-based management of natural resources in Zanzibar*, 2011

59. Anna Rosengren, *Åldrandet och språket: En språkhistorisk analys av hög ålder och åldrande i Sverige cirka 1875–1975*, 2011

60. Emelie Lilliefeldt, *European Party Politics and Gender: Configuring Gender-Balanced Parliamentary Presence*, 2011

61. Ola Svenonius, *Sensitising Urban Transport Security: Surveillance and Policing in Berlin, Stockholm, and Warsaw*, 2011

62. Andreas Johansson, *Dissenting Democrats: Nation and Democracy in the Republic of Moldova*, 2011

63. Wessam Melik, *Molecular characterization of the Tick-borne encephalitis virus: Environments and replication*, 2012

64. Steffen Werther, *SS-Vision und Grenzland-Realität: Vom Umgang dänischer und „volksdeutscher" Nationalsozialisten in Sønderjylland mit der „großgermanischen" Ideologie der SS*, 2012

65. Peter Jakobsson, *Öppenhetsindustrin*, 2012

66. Kristin Ilves, *Seaward Landward: Investigations on the archaeological source value of the landing site category in the Baltic Sea region*, 2012

67. Anne Kaun, *Civic Experiences and Public Connection: Media and Young People in Estonia*, 2012

68. Anna Tessmann, *On the Good Faith: A Fourfold Discursive Construction of Zoroastripanism in Contemporary Russia*, 2012

69. Jonas Lindström, *Drömmen om den nya staden: Stadsförnyelse i det postsovjetisk Riga*, 2012

70. Maria Wolrath Söderberg, *Topos som meningsskapare: Retorikens topiska perspektiv på tänkande och lärande genom argumentation*, 2012

71. Linus Andersson, *Alternativ television: Former av kritik i konstnärlig TV-produktion*, 2012

72. Håkan Lättman, *Studies on spatial and temporal distributions of epiphytic lichens*, 2012

73. Fredrik Stiernstedt, Mediearbete i mediehuset: Produktion i förändring på MTG-radio, 2013

74. Jessica Moberg, *Piety, Intimacy and Mobility: A Case Study of Charismatic Christianity in Present-day Stockholm*, 2013

75. Elisabeth Hemby, *Historiemåleri och bilder av vardag: Tatjana Nazarenkos konstnärskap i 1970-talets Sovjet*, 2013

76. Tanya Jukkala, *Suicide in Russia: A macro-sociological study*, 2013

77. Maria Nyman, *Resandets gränser: Svenska resenärers skildringar av Ryssland under 1700-talet*, 2013

78. Beate Feldmann Eellend, *Visionära planer och vardagliga praktiker: Postmilitära landskap i Östersjöområdet*, 2013

79. Emma Lind, *Genetic response to pollution in sticklebacks: Natural selection in the wild*, 2013

80. Anne Ross Solberg, *The Mahdi wears Armani: An analysis of the Harun Yahya enterprise*, 2013

81. Nikolay Zakharov, *Attaining Whiteness: A Sociological Study of Race and Racialization in Russia*, 2013

82. Anna Kharkina, *From Kinship to Global Brand: The Discourse on Culture in Nordic Cooperation after World War II*, 2013

83. Florence Fröhlig, *A painful legacy of World War II: Nazi forced enlistment: Alsatian/Mosellan Prisoners of war and the Soviet Prison Camp of Tambov*, 2013

84. Oskar Henriksson, *Genetic connectivity of fish in the Western Indian Ocean*, 2013

85. Hans Geir Aasmundsen, *Pentecostalism, Globalisation and Society in Contemporary Argentina*, 2013

86. Anna McWilliams, *An Archaeology of the Iron Curtain: Material and Metaphor*, 2013

87. Anna Danielsson, *On the power of informal economies and the informal economies of power: Rethinking informality, resilience and violence in Kosovo*, 2014

88. Carina Guyard, *Kommunikationsarbete på distans*, 2014

89. Sofia Norling, *Mot "väst": Om vetenskap, politik och transformation i Polen 1989–2011*, 2014

90. Markus Huss, *Motståndets akustik: Språk och (o)ljud hos Peter Weiss 1946–1960*, 2014

91. Ann-Christin Randahl, *Strategiska skribenter: Skrivprocesser i fysik och svenska*, 2014

92. Péter Balogh, *Perpetual borders: German-Polish cross-border contacts in the Szczecin area*, 2014

93. Erika Lundell, *Förkroppsligad fiktion och fiktionaliserade kroppar: Levande rollspel i Östersjöregionen*, 2014

94. Henriette Cederlöf, *Alien Places in Late Soviet Science Fiction: The "Unexpected Encounters" of Arkady and Boris Strugatsky as Novels and Films*, 2014

95. Niklas Eriksson, *Urbanism Under Sail: An archaeology of fluit ships in early modern everyday life*, 2014

96. Signe Opermann, *Generational Use of News Media in Estonia: Media Access, Spatial Orientations and Discursive Characteristics of the News Media*, 2014

97. Liudmila Voronova, *Gendering in political journalism: A comparative study of Russia and Sweden*, 2014

98. Ekaterina Kalinina, *Mediated Post-Soviet Nostalgia*, 2014

99. Anders E. B. Blomqvist, *Economic Natonalizing in the Ethnic Borderlands of Hungary and Romania: Inclusion, Exclusion and Annihilation in Szatmár/Satu-Mare, 1867–1944*, 2014

100. Ann-Judith Rabenschlag, *Völkerfreundschaft nach Bedarf: Ausländische Arbeitskräfte in der Wahrnehmung von Staat und Bevölkerung der DDR*, 2014

101. Yuliya Yurchuck, *Ukrainian Nationalists and the Ukrainian Insurgent Army in Post-Soviet Ukraine*, 2014

102. Hanna Sofia Rehnberg, *Organisationer berättar: Narrativitet som resurs i strategisk kommunikation*, 2014

103. Jaakko Turunen, *Semiotics of Politics: Dialogicality of Parliamentary Talk*, 2015

104. Iveta Jurkane-Hobein, *I Imagine You Here Now: Relationship Maintenance Strategies in Long-Distance Intimate Relationships*, 2015

105. Katharina Wesolowski, *Maybe baby? Reproductive behaviour, fertility intentions, and family policies in post-communist countries, with a special focus on Ukraine*, 2015

106. Ann af Burén, *Living Simultaneity: On religion among semi-secular Swedes*, 2015

107. Larissa Mickwitz, *En reformerad lärare: Konstruktionen av en professionell och betygs-sättande lärare i skolpolitik och skolpraktik*, 2015

108. Daniel Wojahn, *Språkaktivism: Diskussioner om feministiska språkförändringar i Sverige från 1960-talet till 2015*, 2015

109. Hélène Edberg, *Kreativt skrivande för kritiskt tänkande: En fallstudie av studenters arbete med kritisk metareflektion*, 2015

110. Kristina Volkova, *Fishy Behavior: Persistent effects of early-life exposure to 17α-ethiny-lestradiol*, 2015

111. Björn Sjöstrand, *Att tänka det tekniska: En studie i Derridas teknikfilosofi*, 2015

112. Håkan Forsberg, *Kampen om eleverna: Gymnasiefältet och skolmarknadens framväxt i Stockholm, 1987–2011*, 2015

113. Johan Stake, *Essays on quality evaluation and bidding behavior in public procurement auctions*, 2015

114. Martin Gunnarson, *Please Be Patient: A Cultural Phenomenological Study of Haemo-dialysis and Kidney Transplantation Care*, 2016

115. Nasim Reyhanian Caspillo, *Studies of alterations in behavior and fertility in ethinyl estradiol-exposed zebrafish and search for related biomarkers*, 2016

116. Pernilla Andersson, *The Responsible Business Person: Studies of Business Education for Sustainability*, 2016

117. Kim Silow Kallenberg, *Gränsland: Svensk ungdomsvård mellan vård och straff*, 2016

118. Sari Vuorenpää, *Literacitet genom interaction*, 2016

119. Francesco Zavatti, *Writing History in a Propaganda Institute: Political Power and Net-work Dynamics in Communist Romania*, 2016

120. Cecilia Annell, *Begärets politiska potential: Feministiska motståndsstrategier i Elin Wägners 'Pennskaftet', Gabriele Reuters 'Aus guter Familie', Hilma Angered-Strand-bergs 'Lydia Vik' och Grete Meisel-Hess 'Die Intellektuellen'*, 2016

121. Marco Nase, *Academics and Politics: Northern European Area Studies at Greifswald University, 1917–1992*, 2016

122. Jenni Rinne, *Searching for Authentic Living Through Native Faith – The Maausk movement in Estonia*, 2016

123. Petra Werner, *Ett medialt museum: Lärandets estetik i svensk television 1956–1969*, 2016

124. Ramona Rat, *Un-common Sociality: Thinking sociality with Levinas*, 2016

125. Petter Thureborn, *Microbial ecosystem functions along the steep oxygen gradient of the Landsort Deep, Baltic Sea*, 2016

126. Kajsa-Stina Benulic, *A Beef with Meat Media and audience framings of environ-mentally unsustainable production and consumption*, 2016

127. Naveed Asghar, *Ticks and Tick-borne Encephalitis Virus – From nature to infection*, 2016

128. Linn Rabe, *Participation and legitimacy: Actor involvement for nature conservation*, 2017

129. Maryam Adjam, *Minnesspår: Hågkomstens rum och rörelse i skuggan av en flykt*, 2017

130. Kim West, *The Exhibitionary Complex: Exhibition, Apparatus and Media from Kulturhuset to the Centre Pompidou, 1963–1977*, 2017

131. Ekaterina Tarasova, *Anti-nuclear Movements in Discursive and Political Contexts: Between expert voices and local protests*, 2017

132. Sanja Obrenović Johansson, *Från kombifeminism till rörelse: Kvinnlig serbisk organisering i förändring*, 2017

133. Michał Salamonik, *In Their Majesties' Service: The Career of Francesco De Gratta (1613–1676) as a Royal Servant and Trader in Gdańsk*, 2017

134. Jenny Ingridsdotter, *The Promises of the Free World: Postsocialist Experience in Argentina and the Making of Migrants, Race, and Coloniality*, 2017

135. Julia Malitska, *Negotiating Imperial Rule: Colonists and Marriage in the Nineteenth century Black Sea Steppe*, 2017

136. Natalya Yakusheva, *Parks, Policies and People: Nature Conservation Governance in Post-Socialist EU Countries*, 2017

137. Martin Kellner, *Selective Serotonin Re-uptake Inhibitors in the Environment: Effects of Citalopram on Fish Behaviour*, 2017

138. Krystof Kasprzak, *Vara – Framträdande – Värld: Fenomenets negativitet hos Martin Heidegger, Jan Patočka och Eugen Fink*, 2017

139. Alberto Frigo, *Life-stowing from a Digital Media Perspective: Past, Present and Future*, 2017

140. Maarja Saar, *The Answers You Seek Will Never Be Found at Home: Reflexivity, biographical narratives and lifestyle migration among highly-skilled Estonians*, 2017

141. Anh Mai, *Organizing for Efficiency: Essay on merger policies, independence of authorities, and technology diffusion*, 2017

142. Gustav Strandberg, *Politikens omskakning: Negativitet, samexistens och frihet i Jan Patočkas tänkande*, 2017

143. Lovisa Andén, *Litteratur och erfarenhet i Merleau-Pontys läsning av Proust, Valéry och Stendhal*, 2017

144. Fredrik Bertilsson, *Frihetstida policyskapande: Uppfostringskommissionen och de akademiska konstitutionerna 1738–1766*, 2017

145. Börjeson, Natasja, *Toxic Textiles – towards responsibility in complex supply chains*, 2017

146. Julia Velkova, *Media Technologies in the Making – User-Driven Software and Infrastructures for computer Graphics Production*, 2017

147. Karin Jonsson, *Fångna i begreppen? Revolution, tid och politik i svensk socialistisk press 1917–1924*, 2017

148. Josefine Larsson, *Genetic Aspects of Environmental Disturbances in Marine Ecosystems – Studies of the Blue Mussel in the Baltic Sea*, 2017

149. Roman Horbyk, *Mediated Europes – Discourse and Power in Ukraine, Russia and Poland during Euromaidan*, 2017

150. Nadezda Petrusenko, *Creating the Revolutionary Heroines: The Case of Female Terrorists of the PSR (Russia, Beginning of the 20th Century)*, 2017

151. Rahel Kuflu, *Bröder emellan: Identitetsformering i det koloniserade Eritrea*, 2018

152. Karin Edberg, *Energilandskap i förändring: Inramningar av kontroversiella lokaliseringar på norra Gotland*, 2018

153. Rebecka Thor, *Beyond the Witness: Holocaust Representation and the Testimony of Images – Three films by Yael Hersonski, Harun Farocki, and Eyal Sivan*, 2018

154. Maria Lönn, *Bruten vithet: Om den ryska femininitetens sinnliga och temporala villkor*, 2018

155. Tove Porseryd, *Endocrine Disruption in Fish: Effects of 17α-ethinylestradiol exposure on non-reproductive behavior, fertility and brain and testis transcriptome*, 2018

156. Marcel Mangold, *Securing the working democracy: Inventive arrangements to guarantee circulation and the emergence of democracy policy*, 2018

157. Matilda Tudor, *Desire Lines: Towards a Queer Digital Media Phenomenology*, 2018

158. Martin Andersson, *Migration i 1600-talets Sverige: Älvsborgs lösen 1613–1618*, 2018

159. Johanna Pettersson, *What's in a Line? Making Sovereignty through Border Policy*, 2018

160. Irina Seits, *Architectures of Life-Building in the Twentieth Century: Russia, Germany, Sweden*, 2018

161. Alexander Stagnell, *The Ambassador's Letter: On the Less Than Nothing of Diplomacy*, 2019

162. Mari Zetterqvist Blokhuis, *Interaction Between Rider, Horse and Equestrian Trainer – A Challenging Puzzle*, 2019

163. Robin Samuelsson, *Play, Culture and Learning: Studies of Second-Language and Conceptual Development in Swedish Preschools*, 2019

164. Ralph Tafon, *Analyzing the "Dark Side" of Marine Spatial Planning – A study of domination, empowerment and freedom (or power in, of and on planning) through theories of discourse and power*, 2019

165. Ingela Visuri, *Varieties of Supernatural Experience: The case of high-functioning autism*, 2019

166. Mathilde Rehnlund, *Getting the transport right – for what? What transport policy can tell us about the construction of sustainability*, 2019

167. Oscar Törnqvist, *Röster från ingenmansland: En identitetsarkeologi i ett maritimt mellanrum*, 2019

168. Elise Remling, *Adaptation, now? Exploring the Politics of Climate Adaptation through Post-structuralist Discourse Theory*, 2019

169. Eva Karlberg, *Organizing the Voice of Women: A study of the Polish and Swedish women's movements' adaptation to international structures*, 2019

170. Maria Pröckl, *Tyngd, sväng och empatisk timing – förskollärares kroppsliga kunskaper*, 2020

171. Adrià Alcoverro, *The University and the Demand for Knowledge-based Growth The hegemonic struggle for the future of Higher Education Institutions in Finland and Estonia*, 2020

172. Ingrid Forsler, *Enabling Media: Infrastructures, imaginaries and cultural techniques in Swedish and Estonian visual arts education*, 2020

173. Johan Sehlberg, *Of Affliction: The Experience of Thought in Gilles Deleuze by way of Marcel Proust*, 2020

174. Renat Bekkin, *People of reliable loyalty…: Muftiates and the State in Modern Russia*, 2020

175. Olena Podolian, *The Challenge of 'Stateness' in Estonia and Ukraine: The international dimension a quarter of a century into independence*, 2020

176. Patrick Seniuk, *Encountering Depression In-Depth: An existential-phenomenological approach to selfhood, depression, and psychiatric practice*, 2020

177. Vasileios Petrogiannis, *European Mobility and Spatial Belongings: Greek and Latvian migrants in Sweden*, 2020

178. Lena Norbäck Ivarsson, *Tracing environmental change and human impact as recorded in sediments from coastal areas of the northwestern Baltic Proper*, 2020

179. Sara Persson, *Corporate Hegemony through Sustainability – A study of sustainability standards and CSR practices as tools to demobilise community resistance in the Albanian oil industry*, 2020

180. Juliana Porsani, *Livelihood Implications of Large-Scale Land Concessions in Mozambique: A case of family farmers' endurance*, 2020

181. Anders Backlund, *Isolating the Radical Right – Coalition Formation and Policy Adaptation in Sweden*, 2020

182. Nina Carlsson, *One Nation, One Language? National minority and Indigenous recognition in the politics of immigrant integration*, 2021

183. Erik Gråd, *Nudges, Prosocial Preferences & Behavior: Essays in Behavioral Economics*, 2021

184. Anna Enström, *Sinnesstämning, skratt och hypokondri: Om estetisk erfarenhet i Kants tredje Kritik*, 2021

185. Michelle Rydback, *Healthcare Service Marketing in Medical Tourism – An Emerging Market Study*, 2021

186. Fredrik Jahnke, *Toleransens altare och undvikandets hänsynsfullhet – Religion och meningsskapande bland svenska grundskoleelever*, 2021

187. Benny Berggren Newton, *Business Basics – A Grounded Theory for Managing Ethical Behavior in Sales Organizations*, 2021

188. Gabriel Itkes-Sznap, *Nollpunkten. Precisionens betydelse hos Witold Gombrowicz, Inger Christensen och Herta Müller*, 2021

189. Oscar Svanelid Medina, *Att forma tillvaron: Konstruktivism som konstnärligt yrkesarbete hos Geraldo de Barros, Lygia Pape och Lygia Clark*, 2021

190. Anna-Karin Selberg, *Politics and Truth: Heidegger, Arendt and The Modern Political Lie*, 2021

191. Camilla Larsson, *Framträdanden: Performativitetsteoretiska tolkningar av Tadeusz Kantors konstnärskap*, 2021

192. Raili Uibo, *"And I don't know who we really are to each other": Queers doing close relationships in Estonia*, 2021

193. Ignė Stalmokaitė, *New Tides in Shipping: Studying incumbent firms in maritime energy transitions*, 2021

194. Mani Shutzberg, *Tricks of the Medical Trade: Cunning in the Age of Bureaucratic Austerity*, 2021

195. Patrik Höglund, *Skeppssamhället: Rang, roller och status på örlogsskepp under 1600-talet*, 2021

196. Philipp Seuferling, *Media and the refugee camp: The historical making of space, time, and politics in the modern refugee regime*, 2021

197. Johan Sandén, *Närbyråkrater och digitaliseringar: Hur lärares arbete formas av tidsstrukturer*, 2021

198. Ulrika Nemeth, *Det kritiska uppdraget: Diskurser och praktiker i gymnasieskolans svenskundervisning*, 2021

199. Helena Löfgren, *Det legitima ägandet: Politiska konstruktioner av allmännyttans privatisering i Stockholms stad 1990–2015*, 2021

200. Vasileios Kitsos, *Urban policies for a contemporary periphery: Insights from eastern Russia*, 2022

201. Jenny Gustafsson, *Drömmen om en gränslös fred: Världsmedborgarrörelsens reaktopi, 1949–1968*, 2022

202. Oscar von Seth, *Outsiders and Others: Queer Friendships in Novels by Hermann Hesse*, 2022

203. Kristin Halverson, *Tools of the Trade: Medical Devices and Practice in Sweden and Denmark, 1855–1897*, 2022

204. Henrik Ohlsson, *Facing Nature: Cultivating Experience in the Nature Connection Movement*, 2022

205. Mirey Gorgis, *Allt är våld: En undersökning av det moderna våldsbegreppet*, 2022

206. Mats Dahllöv, *Det absoluta och det gemensamma: Benjamin Höijers konstfilosofi*, 2022

207. Anton Poikolainen Rosén, *Noticing Nature: Exploring More Than Human-Centred Design in Urban Farming*, 2022

208. Sophie Landwehr Sydow, *Makers, Materials and Machines: Understanding Experience and Situated Embodied Practice at the Makerspace*, 2022

209. Simon Magnusson, *Boosting young citizens' deontic status: Interactional allocation of rights-to-decide in participatory democracy meetings*, 2022

210. Marie Jonsson, *Vad vilja vegetarianerna? En undersökning av den svenska vegetarismen 1900–1935*, 2022

211. Birgitta Ekblom, *Härskarhyllning och påverkan: Panegyriken kring tronskiftet 1697 i det svenska Östersjöväldet*, 2022

212. Joanna Mellquist, *Policy Professionals in Civil Society Organizations: Struggling for Influence*, 2022

213. David Birksjö, *Innovative Security Business – Innovation, Standardization and ndustry Dynamics in the Swedish Security Sector, 1992–2012*, 2023

214. Roman Privalov, *After space utopia: Post-Soviet Russia and futures in space*, 2023

215. Martin Johansson, *De nordiska lekarna: Grannlandsrelationen i pressen under olympiska vinterspel*, 2023

216. Anna Bark Persson, *Steel as the Answer? Viking Bodies, Power, and Masculinity in Anglophone Fantasy Literature 2006–2016*, 2023